THEIR MISSION:
⊙NE SHOT-⊙NE KILL

U.S. Marine Lance Corporal Craig Roberts. Vietnam, 1965:
We slept during the days and with the fall of night we packed up our rifles and scopes, like shift workers packing a lunch, and went to work. . . . Instead of the hunted, *we* became the hunters hidden in the jungle like ghosts, who killed unseen and then vanished into the bamboo . . .

U.S. Army Sergeant William E. Jones. Normandy, 1944:
With the .30-caliber 1903 Springfield rifle's telescopic sight, I could often find the German snipers hiding in the hedgerows. You couldn't see them with the naked eye, but the 10X scope brought them right out of hiding . . .

U.S. Army Corporal Chet Hamilton. Korea, 1952: In order for the Chicoms to see our troops and fire at them down through their wire as the GIs charged up the hill, they had to lean up and out over their trenches, into view. That was all I needed . . .

U.S. Marine Corporal Tom Rutter. Beirut, 1983: It was like anarchy in which everyone went armed. . . . I crosshaired one of the Shiites who was dragging a dead man. He had been among those who earlier charged from the cafe with rifles blazing. It was an easy shot of about 425 meters. I centered his chest. The bullet slammed him against the side of the car . . .

U.S. Marine Sergeant Carlos Hathcock. Vietnam, 1967:
Both lenses of the enemy sniper's scope, front and back, were shattered. It was obvious what happened. My bullet smashed through his scope and into his right eye. At the moment I shot him, he had his scope trained on me. I just happened to get on the trigger first . . .

ONE SHOT-
ONE KILL

Charles W. Sasser and Craig Roberts

POCKET BOOKS

New York   London   Toronto   Sydney   Tokyo   Singapore

An *Original* Publication of POCKET BOOKS

POCKET BOOKS, a division of Simon & Schuster Inc.
1230 Avenue of the Americas, New York, NY 10020

Copyright © 1990 by Charles W. Sasser and Craig Roberts
Cover art copyright © 1990 Peter Caras

ISBN: 0-671-68219-9

First Pocket Books printing April 1990

10 9 8 7 6 5 4 3 2 1

POCKET and colophon are registered trademarks of
Simon & Schuster Inc.

Printed in the U.S.A.

This book is dedicated to our parents:
Bill and Betty Roberts; George and Mary Wells.
And to Angela Roberts
and Juanita Marie Jackson.

ACKNOWLEDGMENTS

The authors wish to thank the people who made this book possible. Their help in the monumental task of researching and writing this book made a difficult project an enjoyable experience.

Our thanks to:

Colonel Brooke Nihart, USMC, Deputy Director for Marine Corps Museums, and his staff for the invaluable research and documentation provided;

To Lieutenant Colonel J. C. Cuddy, USMC, U.S. Marine Corps Scout/Sniper School, without whose help the contacts and chain of events leading to many interviews would not have been possible;

To Major James Land, USMC (Ret.), for sharing his experiences both in Vietnam and Quantico, Virginia, and for his patience and dedicated assistance throughout the writing;

To Major Dick Culver, USMC (Ret.), for his help in providing information regarding development of the Marine Corps Scout/Sniper School and for lending us his expertise in the area of telescopic sights;

To Staff Sergeant Ronnie Kuykendall, Senior Instructor of the U.S. Army Sniper School, Fort Benning, Georgia, and to his staff for their help in providing the latest information on the U.S. Army Sniper Training Program;

Acknowledgments

To Gunnery Sergeant Carlos N. Hathcock, USMC (Ret.), for all his help, advice, information, and above all for sharing his experiences with the authors after traveling 1,200 miles and taking four days out of his life;

To all the other fine men and their wives who participated in reliving experiences, filling in the gaps in history, and sharing with us the stories that appear on these pages—Sergeant John Fulcher, Sergeant William E. Jones, Private Daniel Webster Cass, Jr., Sergeant Chester Hamilton, Corporal Ernest R. Fish, Corporal Gary Edwards, Corporal Jim Miller, Corporal Ron Szpond, and Corporal Thomas Gregory Rutter;

And, finally, we would like to thank the dozens of other people—sniper instructors, commanding officers, former snipers, librarians, career NCOs, professional marksmen, and others too numerous to list but whose assistance is gratefully acknowledged.

Charles W. Sasser
Craig Roberts

"There survives one lone wolf of the battlefield. He hunts not with the pack. Single-handed, or accompanied by one companion, he seeks cover near the fighting. Sometimes he holes-in behind the tottering walls of a shell-ridden hut, far from the shelter of his lines. Again, at dead of night, he rolls out across the shell-torn fields, burrowing deep into the sodden ground. . . . His game is not to send a hail of rapid fire into a squad or company; it is to pick off with one well-directed, rapidly delivered shot a single enemy. . . ."

U.S. Marine Corps General George O. Van Orden

FOREWORD

The information in this book came from sources ranging from official U.S. Government documents and publications to actual taped interviews with the men whose stories appear on these pages. Brief quotes from knowledgeable individuals came from other sources where their statements were relevant to a given topic. These are: Lones Wigger, quoted from an article in *American Rifleman* magazine ("Good to the Very Last Shot," by Rupp Scott, May 1987); Sergeant Paul Herrman and Captain Tim Hunter, quoted from an article in *Leatherneck* magazine ("Scout Sniper School," by P. L. Thompson, March 1984); and Major D. L. Wright in an article in *Marine Corps Gazette* ("Training the Scout Sniper," by Major D. L. Wright, October 1985).

The chapters in this book dealing with one person and his experiences are based on taped, personal interviews conducted with, and letters written by, the people who volunteered their stories. The vast majority of dialogue appearing in the book was taken from these interviews and letters. In a few instances, dialogue has been recreated based on the interviews to match the situation, action, and personalities, while maintaining factual context as it was presented to the authors.

FOREWORD

If you look at just the statistics, it is damned hard to kill an enemy soldier on the battlefield. During World War II, the Allies fired an average of 25,000 bullets for each enemy soldier they killed. The ratio of bullets to KIAs kept climbing. United Nations troops in Korea expended 50,000 rounds for each dead enemy. In Vietnam, American GIs armed with M-14s at the beginning of the war and, later, with rapid-firing M-16s burned up in excess of 200,000 bullets to get a single body count.

The statistics become even more astonishing if you consider that certain skilled warriors, armed with an unerring eye, infinite patience, and a mastery of concealment and woodcraft, have proved repeatedly that the most deadly weapon on any battlefield is the single, well-aimed shot. In stalking the enemy like big game hunters, these marksmen live out the philosophy that one accurate shot, one bullet costing a few cents, fired with deliberate surgical precision is more deadly and more effective against an enemy than a one-thousand-pound bomb dropped indiscriminately.

Statistically, it takes 1.3 bullets for a trained sniper to kill an enemy.

"There survives one lone wolf of the battlefield," wrote U.S. Marine Corps General George O. Van Orden in a 1940 paper extolling the use of snipers in war. "He hunts not with the pack. Single-handed, or accompanied by one companion, he seeks cover near the fighting. Sometimes he holes-in behind the tottering walls of a shell-ridden hut, far from the shelter of his lines. Again, at dead of night, he rolls out across the shell-torn fields, burrowing deep into the sodden ground. . . . His game is not to send a hail of rapid fire into a squad or company; it is to pick off with one well-directed, rapidly delivered shot a single enemy. . . .

"He is the gadfly of a great war. He must harass the foe. . . . He must hammer relentlessly upon the nerves of the rank and file of the opposing forces, until his rifle crack, joining with others of his kind, becomes a menace more to be feared than the shrieking shells from cannon, or the explosive hail from the mortars. His bullets must come from *nowhere*."

The art and science of sniping is not a product solely of modern warfare. Its roots reach into prehistoric times when man at war saw the advantage of being able to kill his enemy at the farthest possible range with the least danger to himself. Stones launched by slingshots were replaced by spears launched by throwing sticks. The bow and arrow replaced these and was in turn replaced by the crossbow and then by gunpowder. Each technological advancement in weaponry increased the range from which a marksman could hit a target and the accuracy with which he could hit it.

Leonardo da Vinci picked off enemy soldiers from

the walls of besieged Florence with a rifle of his own design at ranges of 300 yards. A sniper hiding in the woods with a crossbow felled Britain's Richard the Lion-Hearted. Lord Admiral Horatio Nelson also became victim of the sniper's simple philosophy of *one shot—one kill*. Early in America's War of Independence, a single bullet could have changed the course of history had a British sniper, Captain Patrick Ferguson, chosen to shoot General George Washington in the back when the general turned and rode away from him at the beginning of the Battle of Brandywine Creek.

To the average western man, who has an aversion to what he considers unsportsmanlike conduct, merely the mention of the word *sniper* evokes an image of an evil little foreign man sneaking through the jungles of Okinawa picking off the good guys, or of a merciless Viet Cong hiding in a tree waiting for the opportunity to kill a 19-year-old GI from Des Moines or Wichita as he walks patrol at Nha Trang. Americans, especially, believe in Gary Cooper or John Wayne who walked down the middle of a dusty street to shoot it out face to face with the bad guys. To bushwhack an enemy, even in war, is considered unfair and underhanded. It is wrong to kill, says western man, but if we do kill we must kill in a fair fight.

Although each war of this century produced a need for snipers, a need that was temporarily filled at places like Salerno and Normandy and Pork Chop Hill and Chu Lai and Beirut, the standard reaction after the need ended was to cork the snipers back into their bottles, as though they never really existed. It was as though we were ashamed of them and what they had done, as though sniping was morally wrong and unfit for a role in the United States armed forces.

If you want to look at it from that point of view, *war*

is immoral. And there is no Gary Cooper or John Wayne in war; if there were, they would be lying dead in the dust of Main Street. In combat, the aim is to survive and to kill before you are killed. The weapon most dreaded on any battlefield is the lone sharp-shooter whose single rifle crack almost invariably means death for the enemy. Hundreds of American GIs and Marines survived because, as General Van Orden put it, "(the sniper's) rifle crack, joining with others of his kind, becomes a menace more to be feared than the shrieking shells from cannon. . . ." American snipers *saved* American lives by killing be-fore the enemy could kill.

Studies show that not every soldier can kill, even in the heat of battle. Even fewer are able to kill calculat-edly, coldly, deliberately, one man at a time, one shot at a time.

"When you look through that rifle scope, the first thing you see is the eyes," said U.S. Marine Captain James Land, a sniper instructor in Vietnam. "There is a lot of difference between shooting at a shadow, shooting at an outline, shooting at a mass, and shoot-ing at a pair of eyes. The first thing that pops out at you through the scope is the eyes. Many men can't do it at that point. It takes a special kind of courage."

Men like U.S. Army Sergeant John Fulcher pos-sessed that rare quality.

Fulcher was a Cherokee Indian from Texas whose sniper platoon dogged the Nazis up the boot of Italy, taking German scalps and striking terror into the hearts of Hitler's troops.

Also, men like:

U.S. Army Sergeant Bill Jones, who hit Utah Beach at Normandy on D-day and rooted out German snipers during the bitter hedgerow fighting that followed;

U.S. Army Sergeant Chet Hamilton, who, at one

setting on Pork Chop Hill in Korea, methodically wiped out forty Chicom soldiers;

U.S. Marine Captain James Land, who helped initiate the sniper program in Vietnam and later worked to launch what is now the best sniper school in the world;

U.S. Marine Sergeant Carlos Hathcock, the most successful sniper in history, whose feats of daring and courage and marksmanship at such places as Elephant Valley and in the General's Camp became legend;

And U.S. Marine Corporal Tom Rutter, who engaged Shiite militiamen in Beirut's "Hooterville."

It was the courage of these men and others like them that has turned the lone wolf of the battlefield into a formidable weapon of romance and controversy. Nowhere is the enemy safe from the sniper's eye. The enemy's life is cheap. It takes only one bullet to kill him.

One shot—one kill.

CHAPTER ONE

U.S. Marine Sergeant
Carlos Hathcock
Vietnam, 1967

For all I know, it might have been a chicken feather, but it earned me a name among the Vietnamese. It was an impulse when I picked it up. I saw a flight of big beautiful white birds flying over against the cloud-streaked red of a setting Asian sun. Somehow, the sight touched me—the beauty of it, the sheer freedom of flight. I picked up a white feather off the ground and stuck it into my bush hat. Everybody carried something for good luck. A coin, a religious medal, even a rabbit's foot. You needed luck if you were a sniper. The hamburgers—the Viet Cong and NVA—started calling me *Long Tràng*. White Feather. North Vietnam offered a bounty of three years' pay to the soldier who plucked that feather from my hat and my head from my shoulders.

Being a sniper was a good job for me. I didn't like killing people—I never liked that—but I liked the job.

I was able to detach myself from everything and do it. I did it to keep our people from getting hurt. I was saving Marine lives. Every hamburger I killed out in Indian Country meant one more Marine or GI would be going back to the World alive. That was how I looked at it.

But I didn't want some hamburger collecting *my* head to save *his* buddies' lives.

I felt a lot safer in the bush than behind the wire on Hill 55. Behind the wire made me uneasy, like a duck must feel on opening day setting on a pond surrounded by hunters. I stood on one of the fingers of the hill and gazed past the concertina and minefields toward the river and the clumps of jungle and bamboo separating the rice paddies. I felt eyes watching me. I couldn't control conditions inside the wire; the hamburgers called the shots. Rockets and mortars had your name written all over them—"To Whom It May Concern." But *out there,* I had control.

I hadn't realized how much impact my hunting had had on the hamburgers until the intel section came up with a wounded Vietnamese woman. The company gunny called me to his hootch to let me know that the *mamasan* was saying the North Vietnamese had detailed an entire sniper platoon to Hill 55 with one primary mission.

"All she could talk about was how they had taken a blood oath not to return home without *Long Tràng's* feather," the gunny said.

That kind of stuff could psych you out, if you let it. I had already seen the circulars passed around in the villages with my picture on them.

"I don't care how hard them hamburgers think they are," I replied, "there ain't none of them hard enough to get me."

"You ain't Superman, Hathcock."

"I never said I was. They'd kill me in a heartbeat if I let down my guard. But the harder they hunt me, the harder I get."

A wrinkle showed between the gunny's eyes. He rubbed a calloused hand across his short-cropped gray hair.

"Hathcock?" He cleared his throat. "From what she says, they may have an ol' *boy* out there that's even better than you."

I didn't say anything.

"All this guy does is live in the bush," the gunny said. "He lives off rats and snakes and worms—shit like that. He claims it'll give him an edge. The woman said this guy catches cobras with his bare hands and eats 'em raw."

"I've spent a lot of time crawling around in the woods too."

The gunny stood up. He still looked sober.

"I know your reputation, Hathcock, but take this for what it's worth. Keep your head down, lad."

I liked being behind the wire even less after that. The NVA sniper platoon started causing damage on the hill. At least one of them did. This hamburger sneaked in to a cluster of low knolls across the valley from Hill 55 and picked off a Marine every chance he got. His shots came at different hours of the day and night, sometimes at dawn, sometimes at dusk, or at noon. He never fired more than one shot a day and never from the same location twice. He was good. It was seven hundred meters across the valley, and he was hitting what he shot at. He killed a sergeant walking past in front of my hootch. My spotter, Corporal Johnny Burke, who accompanied me on most missions to help spot targets and direct fire, wondered if the round had been intended for me—if he *knew* which was my hootch.

It had to be the Cobra sniper. None other would have been so bold.

I studied the terrain. You never knew when he would come. He waited a day between shots, or he waited a week. Some of our snipers tried to get a stand on him, pick him off as he came in and out, but they never saw him. I decided he must have a secret route that brought him into the knolls. He delivered his shot. Then he vanished. He was good. He was making me uneasy. I knew he had to go.

"The next time that hamburger plinks at us," I told Burke, "we're going after his ears."

A few days later, as the shadows were starting to lengthen across the valley, a Marine collapsed as he was scurrying between his sandbagged position on the edge of the hill and one of the hootches farther back. He was already on the ground kicking and groaning by the time the distant report of the gunshot reached the hill.

I always kept my gear ready. "Let's go," I said to Burke. I grabbed my war belt laden with canteen, ammo belt, and knife, and plucked my Winchester Model 70 from just inside the door of my hootch.

It took us an hour to cut the hamburger's trail. It was faint: some flattened grass, a broken weed, an indentation in the soil. I kept glancing at the failing sun as we slowly dogged the trail. Not much time. The spoor led us low beyond the grassy knolls directly to the water of a narrow canal filled with scummy water and leeches and overgrown like a watery tunnel with knife grass and cattails. The trail ended there.

I glanced at Burke. His gaunt face filled with a kind of reluctant admiration for the Cobra's stealth. This was how he was slipping in and out to do his work—float in, float out.

It would be getting dark. Shadows were already thickening in the watery tunnel. I glanced at Burke again. There was no turning back.

I waded into the warm water. The weak current sucked at my waist as we cautiously slid downstream, our eyes adjusting to the shadows. We stopped often to listen. I didn't think the hamburger would be watching his back trail this near his hide, but you learned never to underestimate your foes. We listened, slipped through the water soundlessly, listened some more.

It wasn't long before broken grass and weeds told us where something large had slithered out of the canal. I felt relieved. We picked up the trail and followed it up a wooded ridge. I looked back. Since we had taken to the canal, a thick clot of black clouds had risen to mask the setting sun. The monsoon clouds were moving; you could see the demarcation between night and the last of day as the clouds swiftly escorted in darkness. In no time the first big drops began to fall.

Talking was not necessary. Burke and I had been together in the bush too much to need words. We just looked at each other and burrowed like rats into a thicket where we rolled into our ponchos to wait for daybreak. The rain drummed on the forest leaves and closed in our world to the size of what you could feel within arm's reach.

Dawn painted a clear sky orange. We stirred. Morning toiletries consisted of taking a leak, adding some fresh camouflage paint to our faces. It was all done in complete silence. Then we picked up the sniper's trail again. Rain filtered by jungle canopies falls softly and gently on the forest floor, no matter how it savages the upper levels. It had not destroyed the spoor we followed.

In no time we came upon a small clearing in the jungle. We lay on our bellies concealed in the bush, watching. The sniper's trail led to a small hand-dug cave in the center of the clearing. The opening faced us. The cave contained a sleeping bed of dried grass. As far as I could determine there was only one way in and out of the cave. It made me suspect a trap. The trail was too clearly marked going in for it to be anything else.

The clearing was in the shape of a big circle less than one hundred meters across. A ridge beyond jutted out of the forest. It overlooked the clearing. If the Cobra was keeping an eye on his back trail—and I felt sure he was—then that was where he would be. Although I studied the ridge foot by foot through field glasses, I detected nothing suspicious. There was just the lush green of the jungle dripping water from last night's rain.

We proceeded more cautiously. Hunting men, you develop a kind of sixth sense. My sixth sense told me the Cobra was near. He was cunning and clever—and he wanted the white feather in my hat.

Crawling on our bellies, we circled the clearing and made for the ridge. Soon, we approached a narrow draw at its base. The draw was filled with birds all busily feeding on the ground. The sniper had sprinkled rice to attract birds as an early warning signal in case his trap in the clearing didn't work.

I had a feeling that the first man who spotted the other would be the one to claim the kill. Thinking quickly, I tossed a tree branch into the feeding birds to let the hamburger know his ruse had not worked. The birds lifted in a raucous cloud. Knowing we were on to him, the hamburger abandoned his hide on the ridge top. We heard him scrambling down the ridge into the draw at the opposite end from us.

Then the birds settled and the only sound we heard was water droplets falling from the trees. The Cobra sniper was waiting. Burke was breathing a little deeper than normal as the stalk began. At the moment, it was unclear exactly who was stalking whom.

It was slow going.

Midafternoon found Burke and me with the high ground. Clawing slowly up the side of the ridge, we topped it, then came to a saddle that overlooked both the cave clearing and the draw. Our end of the draw cut through the saddle below us while the sniper's end disappeared ahead of us in a clotting of undergrowth and jumbled moss-covered boulders. I suspected the Cobra had picked his way through a thicket of thorn bushes on our right flank and was hiding somewhere beyond, as patient as we. While we glassed for him, he was undoubtedly scanning for us with his scope.

The sun beat down hard on our backs. It had already steamed away most of last night's moisture. Sweat stung my eyes. I tried to keep it wiped away. Seeing wasn't just important; right now, it was *everything*.

The top of the ridge was sparsely vegetated. I inched my way through the sunlight to the roots of a large tree. I hoped to get a better view from behind the tree's shadows. As soon as I was in place, Burke started across the square of open light, using his fingers and toes like claws.

When something happens, it happens suddenly. The crack of a shot caught my breath in its echo. My head snapped toward Burke. I knew he was dead. Instead, he was behind the tree next to me by the time the reverberations died and I heard the sniper crashing through the forest as he changed positions. He swept over the opposite end of the ridge and down the other side.

Then the sun beat down again on more silence.

"Carlos, I'm hit!" Burke whispered frantically. "The bastard shot me in the ass!"

I took a look.

"That's not blood. It's water. The hamburger shot a hole in your canteen."

Burke managed a sheepish grin.

When he recovered and stopped trembling, we ran in short, bursting charges, each covering the other, to the top of the ridge above the saddle where it looked down into a brush-choked gully sloping off the ridge to the forest. Beyond the forest began the rice paddies studded with grass-topped Vietnamese hootches. A farmer and his water buffalo were plowing in one field, oblivious to the drama being played out in the jungle.

We lay behind cover, waiting and scanning the gully for movement. The Cobra had made the first shot; we couldn't afford to let him have a second.

"He's still there," I whispered. "I can feel him."

Three years' pay made it worth his taking chances.

We remained motionless for an hour. Dark clouds began gathering on the horizon for another night's monsoon. The sun rode lower in a brassy sky, crossing on our right flank to our backs where it shone hard and bright down the gully into the watching eyes of our hamburger. It became our ally.

The standoff continued.

The first man who stirred before nightfall became the other's kill.

Into the second hour of the impasse, with the strain and tension increasing with the passing minutes, I detected a flash of light deep in the gully. It caught my scope and I held it. Burke had the field glasses.

"What do you make of it?" I asked him.

He looked, scowling.

"It almost looks like someone's flashing a mirror or something."

I experienced a strange feeling. It started at my toes and left my body chilled. Although I never *chanced* a shot, always preferring to wait until I was sure of a target, I suddenly knew that if I didn't shoot now I'd never have another opportunity. It had to be that sixth sense working.

Cross-hairing the glimmer of reflected light, still unable to determine what it was, knowing only that in these surroundings it was something unnatural, I took up trigger slack.

The bark of the Winchester Model 70 shrieked down the gully, shattering the quiet that had endured since the Cobra killed Burke's canteen. Next to me, I felt Burke give an involuntary start as the end of the gully two hundred yards from us exploded. There was no mistaking where the 30.06 slug caught the sniper. The body of a man shot through the head often flops around like a chicken with its neck wrung, the brain gone haywire, shooting all the nerves in the body with its electricity before the lights go out permanently.

The Cobra sniper's arms and legs flailed and thrashed. His body repeatedly propelled itself into the air, blood spurting, as it cleared a red-smeared nest in the bushes. It arched its torso against the sky; the entire body began trembling desperately until life was simply gone and the thing that had been a man minutes ago collapsed to earth.

Burke was the first one to him. He picked up the dead sniper's rifle and stared at it.

"*Holy shit!* Nobody's gonna believe this!"

Both lenses of the scope, front and back, were shattered. I examined the dead hamburger. It was obvious what had happened. My bullet smashed through his scope and into his right eye. At the moment I shot him, the Cobra had his scope trained on me and was a hairbreadth away from claiming the bounty on my head.

I just happened to get on the trigger first.

It was a sobering thought.

CHAPTER TWO

It was Sergeant Carlos Hathcock who combined within one man all the physical, psychological, and mental traits associated with success as a combat sniper. Reared in the rural areas of Arkansas, Tennessee, and Louisiana, a region that has produced many military sharpshooters, including Sergeant Alvin York, Hathcock already knew how to shoot when he enlisted in the U.S. Marine Corps in 1959 on his seventeenth birthday. After polishing his skills over the next several years in Marine marksmanship competition, winning numerous championships, including the highly coveted Wimbledon Cup, he went to Vietnam and walked off Hill 55 and into the nightmares of the Viet Cong. He made 93 confirmed kills and at least 200 others that were not "confirmed" but were dead anyhow. In order for a kill to be confirmed it had to be witnessed by someone other than the sniper—preferably by an officer or NCO. Legends of *Long Tràng* and his daring and skill spread among both friendlies and enemy. The Vietnamese heard his name with

17

dread. Whenever *Long Tr'ang* showed up somewhere, it was a foregone conclusion that someone, soon, was going to die.

Uniquely gifted as he was as a sniper, perhaps the most successful ever in the bloody business of shooting down enemies one at a time, Carlos Hathcock merely followed a tradition that extended in America at least as far back as the Indian fighters on the colonial frontier and Colonel Daniel Morgan's "shirtmen" of the Revolutionary War.

Marksmanship was an honored skill on the frontier. The deadly aim of Daniel Boone and Davy Crockett was the stuff of legend. Where the Americans went, ever westward, so went the rifle and with it the rifleman's skill at hitting what he shot at. Andrew Jackson recognized this skill when he sent out snipers to harass the advance of the British on New Orleans. Hiram Berdan acknowledged it when, under the direction of General Winfield Scott, he recruited the "United States Sharpshooters" to use against the Confederates. The Confederates retaliated at places like Gettysburg where their own rifleman snipers knocked down General Vincent and General Weed, among other officers. Teddy Roosevelt recruited his "Rough Riders" based largely on their skills with a long gun.

The static trench warfare of World War I, the Great War, elevated sniping and sharpshooting to the common method of fighting as enemies contrived to pick off each other without being picked off in return. An American who enlisted with the Canadians to fight with the English in France formulated the sniper's skills into a science that was to be used and expanded upon in training American military snipers up to the present Army sniper and U.S. Marine scout/sniper schools. Captain Herbert W. McBride might well be considered the father of the modern sniper's science and art. He wrote the textbook on the subject garnered from his combat experiences in the trenches, accounts of which he kept in a logbook:

> *December 1st. Hazy—near leaning tree. 1 shot. Fell, and they pulled him in. Two shots at helpers—got one.*
> *December 7th. Brt & clear. Fresh SW wind. Twice men showed themselves. Three shots, sure of one. 50 yards R. one man—one shot. Artillery blew down MG emplacement showing open end of covered trench. Men trying to get out. 4 shots, 2 known hits. Thirty yards left, 1 man, 1 shot. Got him. This was a good day.*
> *December 9th. Shot (one and) three successive helpers. All four lying in sight at dark.*
> *December 16th. Clear. Fine hunting. 16 good shots—7 known hits and feel sure of at least four more.*

Armed with a special Ross rifle and a telescopic sight, McBride kept notes on how ballistics were affected by such externals as temperature, humidity, wind, and other changes in weather and lighting conditions. He improved upon techniques of camouflage and concealment. He developed methods of fooling the enemy about the sniper's exact location. For example, he learned that a rifle bullet fired past a tree or building or rock made a sonic crack in passing that confused the enemy by sounding as though it came from that location instead of from the sniper's true hide. All these techniques were passed on and used not just by American snipers but by military marksmen around the world. When Captain James Land started his sniper school in Vietnam, he depended upon the passed-down knowledge from a sniper who practiced his craft a half century before.

The reasons American military riflemen after World War II made such a poor showing in marksmanship skills, resulting in the dramatic rise in the ratio of shots fired to KIAs obtained, may be due to the rapid urbanization of American society and a tendency for the peacetime U.S. military to relax its soldierly skills. Industrialization simply reduced drastically the number of men who *needed* to use firearms either for defense or to supplement the table. And the fact that GIs in Vietnam often referred to their snipers as *Murder Incorporated* illustrates the old American attitude that it is unfair to shoot an enemy from hiding. It was not until after the Vietnam war that the Marine Corps established a full-time sniper school; the Army followed in 1987.

All through American history, the art and science of sniping has been virtually neglected during peacetime. Inhibitions against snipers got set aside when war came—"In battle, the only bullets that count are those that hit," Theodore Roosevelt observed—but they quickly returned once the need was gone.

After Pearl Harbor, the American military saw the need when GIs found themselves hurled against an enemy who had no such inhibitions. From the jungles of Guadalcanal to the honeycombed ridges of Okinawa, the Japanese employed snipers to harass and delay the American advance. Marines falling to sniper bullets proved that in war, snipers count far out of proportion to their actual numbers.

In Europe, the Germans begrudged the Allies every turn in the bloody, torturous road to Berlin. The struggle from Salerno to Rome became the longest and bitterest campaign of the war. Nazi snipers made the

Allies pay in blood and sweat for every mile of advance.

The hedgerows of Normandy following D-day were terrifying places. Nazi defenders dug in among the hedgerows were virtually impervious to fire. A single machine gun in a hedgerow mowed down troops as they attacked from one hedge to another. Snipers mounted on wooden platforms in treetops picked off attackers two and three fields over.

Out of necessity, Americans initiated their own sniper programs to counter Japanese marksmen in the Pacific and Germans in Europe. Little uniformity existed in these programs in how snipers were selected and trained, even from battalion to battalion. While a number of sniper schools were set up, both stateside and in occupied territory, some gave five weeks of intensive training and others offered a day's familiarization before shipping the "snipers" to the front. Many units made no pretense of sniper training; they merely selected those who shot the highest scores on the rifle range and dubbed them with the title.

"Sniper?" puzzled one soldier. "What the hell does a sniper *do?*"

The best of these marksmen, whether school trained or simply designated, came from the American Southwest where lanky farm boys grew up as wild as the jack rabbits and deer they pursued year around, or they came from the hill country of Arkansas, Tennessee, Virginia, and Kentucky. Barefooted with floppy hats or wearing dusty runover boots, they were crack shots with their rusty old .22s and .30-.30s long before they ever saw a 1903 Springfield or an M-1 Garand.

They suffered tremendous casualties. Fifth Army snipers in Italy lost up to 80 percent of their number to hostile fire. The Twenty-fourth Marine Division had nine snipers alive out of an original twenty-four when the Battle of Iwo Jima ended. Sniper squad sergeants had to go around recruiting replacements.

"You in pretty good shape?" Army Sergeant John Fulcher asked a prospect.

The fighting from Salerno on the march toward Rome left him short nearly half his squad.

"I ran track in high school."

"Is that a fact? Do you smoke?"

"Never could stand it."

"Do you drink?"

"Well, I ain't no drunk if that's what you're getting at."

"Where you from?"

"Arkansas originally. Now I'm from Lubbock, Texas."

"That a fact? Boy, can you *shoot?*"

"I'm an ol' squirrel hunter, Sergeant."

"A fact? Congratulations, boy. You're a *sniper.*"

The sniper school that became the model for future schools in both the Army and Marines sprang up from the hills north of San Diego, California, in January 1943. The first commander of the Marine Corps Scout and Sniper School at Green's Farm was USMC Lieutenant Claude N. Harris, who seated his sniper recruits underneath the eucalyptus trees in the front yard of the old farmhouse turned school headquarters and growled, "Snipers can save a country. Look what they're doing for Russia."

A fifteen-year veteran of the Corps, Harris was a mustang who climbed through the enlisted ranks to an officer's commission. During his USMC career, he had fought in the Haitian and Nicaraguan campaigns and had fired on seven championship Marine Corps rifle teams. In 1935 he won the National Rifle Championship. The Corps brought him back from a combat outpost in the Pacific to organize and command the new academy for killers. Rugged but mild-mannered, appreciating the value of the single well-aimed shot, he became the ideal boss for the gangs of expert riflemen his school turned out every five weeks.

Saying it wasn't enough for a sniper to be able to plink a round into a stationary target at four or five hundred yards, Harris built upon the experiences of previous snipers like Captain McBride to mold a human weapon who could shoot well, but who could also find his way around on the battlefield and survive. His five-week course included training in map reading, sketching, aerial photo reading, the use of the compass, camouflage, construction of sniper hides, individual concealment, stalking, and, of course, long-range shooting.

Spending most days in the field, Marine students scattered into the surrounding canyons where they crawled through barbed wire entanglements, dug hasty field fortifications, made range estimates, and drew maps from memory. They did a lot of scouting—"silent walking"—over rough terrain. One of their tests was to lie in total darkness and estimate the number of men in a passing patrol by the sound of their footfalls.

In the mornings and afternoons, using 1903 Springfields and modified Garands, the students fired at man-silhouette targets set at various ranges up to five hundred yards. Snap-firing at disappearing and moving targets managed by wires, they learned how to hold at any range. The final week was devoted almost exclusively to telescopic long-range firing.

At the same time that Green's Farm was teaching the value of making each shot count, the Marine Corps combat philosophy continued to follow the tradition of using mass firepower. That philosophy called for the Navy to blast hell out of a target, then a division or so of Marines swarmed ashore to overwhelm the enemy with sheer guts and gunfire. Many high-ranking officers remained skeptical of devoting so much time, money, and energy to a relatively few marksmen when what the war really needed was more riflemen on the front lines. Ignoring what the Japanese could do with snipers, these officers commonly underestimated the effectiveness of trained sharpshooters.

Two such officers visited Green's Farm early in the autumn of 1943 to inspect training. Harris gave them a fast ride in his jeep through the desert brush to an upland pasture about three miles from the farmhouse. The pasture—actually the floor of a canyon—was covered with boulders and bushes browned by the summer's sun. Nothing was in sight except for a tiny, weathered shack and a buzzard sitting on a little tree about 150 yards away.

"Well, sirs," Harris said. "We can now look over a class in creeping and crawling."

The inspectors, a colonel and a major, looked up and down the canyon and across the pasture. They looked at each other. They looked at Harris.

"I suppose you mean the class will be along presently?" the colonel said.

Harris grinned. "No, sir. They're out there right now."

He gave a signal. The startled buzzard took to the air as two Marines in camouflage sprang from the brush only a few yards in front of the surprised visitors. Another helmeted trooper snaked out of a skillfully concealed spider trap about three feet away. Other Marines popped up from behind boulders and bushes all over the pasture.

As the astonished officers continued to watch, Marines crept and crawled over the hot rocks and sparse, thorny terrain for a thousand yards without being spotted. They slipped stealthily down the canyon, snap-firing accurately at disappearing targets. They lay on their bellies or slung themselves aloft in scrubby trees to pick off distant targets using telescopic sights.

When the demonstration ended, Harris let the officers' silence measure out a span of time. Suddenly, the colonel, whose mouth hung open, emitted a loud whoop.

"Goddamn!" he shouted. "Give me just one battalion of Marines like these and I can take Tokyo *and* Berlin!"

CHAPTER THREE

U.S. Army Sergeant
John Fulcher
Italy, 1943—44

The drill instructor's plate-brimmed hat rested on the bridge of his nose.

"Boy!" he barked.

"Yes, sir."

"What's your name, boy?"

"John Fulcher, sir."

"Hellfire, boy, I ain't no 'sir.' I work for a living. Can't you see? I'm a sergeant. You know how to shoot, John Fulcher?"

"I can shoot an acorn outa the top of an ol' oak tree with a .22."

"Can you now? You an Injun, huh? You ever scalp any white men?"

"Not yet I ain't, Sergeant."

The green recruits of the Thirty-sixth Division, Texas Army National Guard, fidgeted in the Texas sun and dust of that fall of '42 at Camp Bowie. We were rough-looking farm boys in scuffed brogans repaired with baling wire, faded overalls, and cambray work shirts. I was a wiry six-footer in the first ranks, then twenty-five years old, with the black hair and coppery skin of a full-blood Cherokee mother and the lighter-colored eyes of a German-Irish father. I was the first of five brothers to join up.

The DI moved on down the formation, jutted his face into another boy's face.

"Why'd you join up?" he asked.

"To kill me some of them Nazis and Japs."

"Did you now?"

"Yes, Sergeant."

"I promise you a chance at doing just that, boy."

The farm boy's face split into a shy grin.

After boot camp, the sergeant encouraged some of us tougher boys who could shoot a little to volunteer for what he called the scout/snipers. I suppose I *was* one of the tougher ones. I could jog across the flats all day carrying a forty-pound knapsack, and, as for shooting, I still had enough left in me at the end of the run to stalk a wily Texas whitetail buck and bring him down with one shot.

"You the kind of boys we looking for."

You had to *volunteer* for it though. Somebody in ranks muttered that the life expectancy of a sniper in combat was about what you might expect of a snowball dropping in west Texas in July. Whoever said it just stood there in his khakis and stared straight ahead. He wasn't volunteering.

A couple of boys stepped out of ranks. What the hell. I could do it. I gave a shrug and moved forward. The sergeant grinned at me.

"I figured you would, Fulcher," he said.

The sniper school was held right there at camp. What time we weren't running, making forced marches, or stalking each other out in the mesquite, we were shooting on the rifle ranges. A lot of shooting at targets about five hundred yards away. They issued us new M-1Ds still in cosmoline. The D model was an ordinary Garand, except it had a heavy match barrel and flash suppressor, a set action for the trigger so you could get a smoother squeeze and discharge, a leather cheek piece, and a telescopic sight.

The scout/snipers were supposed to operate in six- and twelve-man squads, pushing out ahead of friendly elements, into no-man's-land and sometimes even behind enemy lines. We provided security by being the eyes and ears for the battalion. Whatever the enemy was doing, we found out about it and funneled back the information.

That was the scouting part. The other part was the skirmishing. Wherever we found the enemy—his patrols and squads and lookouts—we picked him off until he was afraid to go where we were.

Before I went overseas, I knew I had the skills to kill a man up to five hundred yards away. What none of us knew, however, was how we'd react when we peered through our scopes for the first time at the face of a man we were going to kill with a press of the finger. You can shoot at bull's-eyes and man outlines all you want, and you can bullshit and act bold and boast about what you're *going* to do, but you'll never know what you've got inside you until the real thing comes. You'll never know if you can do it or not until then.

My Thirty-sixth Division landed at Salerno with three other Allied divisions on September 8, 1943. We were packed into the transports still out to sea when word went around that Italy had surrendered. We thought that meant the landing was called off. Everybody in the crowded holds ran around cheering and slapping each other on the backs with relief. The celebration proved a bit premature. A deathly silence crept through the bays when we learned we were still going in, when the guns on the cruisers and destroyers opened up to soften up the beach for us. The Italians might have sloped off into the night ahead of the invasion, but the Germans moved in to fill up the positions.

It took about a week for the Allies to fight their way off the landing. We snipers waited until after the first waves secured the beachhead before we went ashore with headquarters. From the rails on the transport decks, we watched the smoke boil up from the battle while the clamor of it pounded around us, deafening us like sticking your head underneath a washtub while about two dozen bullies pounded on it with clubs. Even after we were on land, there wasn't much for us to do except keep our heads down until we broke out and started the long push to Rome. That was when the snipers went into action.

As the krauts withdrew to set up another defense, they left delaying elements behind. We made them dread us. One single shot would ring out from a ridge or hilltop. *One* shot. Generally, an officer—or somebody in the ranks if we couldn't tell the officer— dropped like a sack of rotten potatoes. That was called "establishing a presence." The Nazis knew we were always out there, but they never knew where we were or when we would strike next. It had to make life hellish for them.

Like I said, you never knew what you'd do when you had your first enemy in your sights until the time came. I found out shortly after we climbed into the hills surrounding Salerno. I dropped off from my squad in the bush and wriggled into a hide where I waited alone, scoping out the side of a hill opposite me. The hill fell off into a narrow brown valley bisected by a dry stream bed below. It was a clear, fine morning with good shooting light and no wind.

An enemy patrol of five or six cut through the head-high brush on the opposite rise. The range was at least seven hundred yards, too far away to be sure of a hit. I let the patrol pass. It angled up through the brush, then turned and followed a draw out of sight. Watching, I felt tense, but I was more excited than nervous or scared. It was a little like hunting deer in the piñon pine country of Texas. The terrain even reminded me of parts of Texas.

I heard birds fluttering in the bush, small animals scurrying. If you grew up outdoors, you knew the difference between the movements of animals and man.

I waited, lulled into a false sense of security by the feeling of peace and isolation that settled over the valley. The sun was warm. Insects hummed. I kept scanning the hillside with my scope, not really expecting to find anything now.

Suddenly, my scope filled. I felt my heart race. It was a shock like when you have just spotted the biggest buck of your life. The German was young and slim and had his helmet pulled low, almost like he was trying to hide underneath it. He was no more than one hundred yards away as he slipped through the brush, stopping every so often to look around, like a coyote advancing on a henhouse. I figured him the point man on a patrol.

Spellbound, I watched as he tucked his rifle underneath his arm so he could use both hands to undo his fly. I was careful not to make any sudden movements. That spooks a man same as a deer.

I became aware that my sight picture through the scope was blurred. My hands were trembling, jiggering the scope. I forced myself to take a deep silent breath and let it out slowly to settle my nerves, like they taught in sniper school. Feeling more calm afterwards, I zeroed in on the German and took up trigger slack. I was going to make a heart shot. The sight picture in the optics jumped at me bright and clean. It showed a human being in an altogether human act—taking a leak.

My rifle began to shake.

Jesus God! Settle down.

I remembered it had been like this when, as a kid, I shot my first buck. After the first time, it was all right.

But there was a difference between then and now. *That* had been a *deer.*

I willed my breathing to slow down. I forced my hands steady. He wouldn't be standing there forever taking a leak, a perfect stationary target. With more effort, I detached my mind from its conscience. The German was starting to shake himself off. He was looking around again. I couldn't recall my mouth ever having felt like the skin of a horned toad before.

I squeezed the trigger.

Sonofabitch!

The German bounced into the air like a startled Texas jack rabbit and took off through the brush like the hounds were right on his ass.

I tried to lead him in the scope, but he flickered in and out of the picture. That German could *run.* Exasperation pulled my trigger for me, and kept pulling it until the expended clip *pinged* from the rifle's receiver. I shot hell out of a half acre of terrain, but the German vanished into the brush. If even one bullet so much as nipped his hide, it wasn't evident from the way his legs were carrying him up the side of that hill.

I vowed the next time it would be different. No more buck fever.

* * *

We snipers adopted a tactic the Nazis sometimes used. Slipping from our lines before daylight, we located a hill or ridge within range of a road or trail inside enemy-occupied territory, divided it into sectors for each two-man team—sniper and spotter—and then settled down to wait for whatever came along.

I was hiding among a jumble of boulders high on the side of a ridge that offered me an escape route out the back. The sun came up and bathed the broad valley below in soft morning light. A dirt road wound through the short brown grass and among a scattering of leafless trees. It failed to miss a number of shell craters.

I spotted troops coming at the end of the road where it hazed into the horizon. I nudged my partner and nodded in their direction. We continued to squint into the sun as the troops became individual soldiers marching in company formation, like they were in a Berlin parade for the *Fuehrer* or something. Through binoculars, I could tell they were green replacements. Their uniforms were still a crisp gray green; their jackboots kicking up little spurts of dust still shone. They left a cloud of dust hanging in their wake. Apparently, they were on their way to the front.

I looked at my partner. He had his rifle scope trained on them. He looked back at me. He shook his head.

A *whole* company?

Peering through my rifle scope, I could see the oily glisten of sweat on the commander's brow. Most of the time you could tell the officers. They wore sidearms and were always shouting and waving their arms.

I never much liked officers anyhow.

I nodded at my partner. *Let's take them. They're green. Even if they organized an assault, we could be gone off the ridge before they got halfway across the field to us.*

My hands remained as steady as when I shot my second deer. As cool as could be, I cross-haired the officer and shot him through the belly. He looked momentarily surprised. He plopped down on his butt in the middle of the road. The report of the shot reached him as he fell over onto his back. He was dead by the time I brought my rifle down out of recoil and picked him up again in my scope. His legs were drumming on the road, but he was dead. His body just didn't know it yet.

The other krauts were so green they didn't know enough to scatter for cover until my partner got in his licks by knocking down one more. Even then, they behaved more like quail than combat troops. They hid in the drainage ditches and in some shell craters, their heads bobbing up. Just like quail. I figured I could have drilled two or three more, but I held my fire. It wouldn't do to be pinpointed, even by green troops.

Ordinarily, we would have slipped down over the other side of the ridge and put some distance between them and us before they sent out patrols. But I was curious about this bunch. I wanted to see what they'd do.

After a short while, when there were no more shots, a junior officer in the ditch rose cautiously to one knee. Shading his eyes, he stared at the ridge in the *opposite* direction from where we were hiding. He gradually gained confidence when still nothing happened. He stood up and looked around. He carried a Mauser. He walked out into the road and stood a moment and looked at the two dead men. That seemed to do something to him. Turning suddenly, he ran back to the ditch and started flapping his arms and haranguing his cowering soldiers. Finally, the fearful replacements clambered to their feet.

The company reorganized without making an attempt to find us. It tore off down the road again toward the front, although, this time, the soldiers spaced themselves at greater intervals and marched with their weapons at the ready. They left their dead lying sprawled in the road beneath the sun. A truck would be along after awhile to pick them up.

As soon as the Germans swept around a distant bend in the road, they were greeted by the twin *Crack! Crack!* of two more rifle shots as they entered another Yank team's sector. I figured the junior officer was probably dead this time.

After I killed the officer in the road, I felt something inside me start to change. When you go into combat you revert to the most vicious kind of animal that ever walked the earth. You become a predator. I got to where it hurt me more to kill a good dog than a human being.

It was slow going through Italy. Cold settled in, the type of wet, bone-chilling cold that comes with drizzling rain. Hitler's troops bogged down, and we bogged down at their throats. The dogfaces huddled miserably underneath their ponchos or whatever shelter they could find and cursed the war and the weather and each other. The snipers didn't have that kind of luxury. We were always out ahead, our job to keep the jerries nervous worrying about which of them we'd get next.

I made sergeant and that moved me up to sniper squad leader. The promotion was a matter of attrition; the former sergeant caught one. Half the boys in the sniper squad were Indians, including two Sioux from the Black Hills. I overheard some of the other GIs referring to us as "savages." They said, "The war party's going out scalping." They said it in admiration, and that's the way we took it. After all, our ancestors *had* fought the way we snipers were fighting now.

Word came that the Germans executed on the spot any Yank sniper, *or* Indian, they captured. They were that unnerved by us.

One afternoon, my six-man patrol was scouting a road through the woods in no-man's-land when the point man spotted a German snooping toward us along the same road. He gave the danger signal and we got down behind cover in the bushes. The kraut hadn't seen us. If he kept coming, he would pass directly in front of us. For some reason, men aren't as alert and observant on dreary days as they are when the sun is shining.

I pointed to one of the Sioux and drew the palm of my hand across my throat. He nodded. Instantly, his hatchet appeared in his hand and he slithered through the brush like a snake until he came to some thick undergrowth growing almost into the road. The unsuspecting kraut kept coming, shuffling along in a sort of weary dogtrot, his head bobbing. I figured he was the advance scout for an element that would be following shortly. We had to work fast.

My Sioux kept his hatchet so sharp he was always amazing the other GIs by shaving hair off their arms with it. He waited perfectly still until the German came bobbing up, his jackboots crunching gravel. I saw the kraut's face; he hadn't shaved in awhile. Put him in GI fatigues and you couldn't have distinguished him from our own tired and shaggy grunts. The Indian sprang into the road behind the soldier with his hatchet and severed the kraut's spinal cord just below his neck. The Sioux ducked a geyser of blood as the body toppled, but some of it still sprayed his face. The body was still twitching when the Sioux dragged it to us in the bushes.

It was just like I figured. I glimpsed the dead man's element in gray green uniforms hiking along beyond where the road curved and then stretched out across a brown plain. The Germans were moving along the road toward the front, seemingly confident that their scout would give them warning of any danger.

A thought struck me.

"Scalp the sonofabitch," I said, pointing at the dead jerry.

The Sioux knifed a thin line around the head from the brow and above the ears to the back of the neck, and then peeled off the thick hair like peeling an orange. We dragged the warm corpse next to the road, propped it against a tree, and folded its hands in its lap. From a short distance away, he looked as though he had just stopped to rest. He looked like he was wearing a red skull cap. He looked good sitting there while my squad and I hid in the woods and waited.

The other Germans rounded the bend in the road and came tramping up. The first one to spot the dead soldier stopped like he had collided with an invisible wall. His rifle swung to the ready. He seemed uncertain. I could almost see him blinking. He stuck out his face to get a better look as the others crowded around. They jabbered like a bunch of starlings in a bare elm.

One of them called the dead man's name. When he failed to respond, the entire bunch advanced, their eyes riveted on the spectacle. When they were near, their faces shattered in the sudden terror of recognition.

They still wore those expressions when my squad opened up. We shot down eight of them in the middle of the road. Two escaped. They ran off down the road in the direction they'd come from. I let them go to spread the word.

When the next Germans came along, they found nine of their soldiers, all scalped, sitting neatly like ducks in a row alongside the road with their hands folded in their laps. I figured their Teutonic fondness for order would have appreciated that.

Later, much later, when times were normal again, all this bothered me. I woke up sometimes sweating from nightmares. But for that time, in that place, killing was an everyday fact of life. Once, outside some village, my squad and I were resting on a hillside overlooking our company dug in among the trees next to a road when a pretty young Italian woman came along riding her bicycle. She waved each time she approached a group of GIs, who naturally waved back at her. But as soon as she passed, German mortar shells rained down on the Americans. It was obvious what the girl was doing. She was pinpointing targets for Nazi artillery spotters in the hills.

I sighed and nodded at one of my Sioux. He took bead and knocked her dead off the bicycle. Later, another Italian came out and stole her bicycle, but it was two days before somebody came for the body.

That was the way it was. Scalping an enemy was nothing if you could take bead on a pretty girl and kill her. Besides, scalping struck fear into the Germans. It made them overcautious and leery about taking chances. If you looked at it that way, scalping was helping to win the war. It saved GI lives.

Sniping was never one-sided. Whenever the desperate Germans fell back from a position, they left their own snipers behind as rear guards. They hid in the bombed-out towns and waited for the Allies to come. Kraut artillery bracketed the open places, while the German snipers hid to cover places the artillery couldn't reach. You got mortared and ran for cover, only to find some jerry sharpshooter plinking at you. The German snipers took a toll of their own against the Allies.

It took a sniper to root out a sniper. Our experience

in the trade helped us locate where the enemy marks-men might be hiding in old churches or in the ground-work maze of bombed-out buildings. Before our troops went in, they called up the snipers and we went over the rubble foot by foot with binoculars. Some-times, if it looked like cockroaches in the destruction because the snipers were so busy, we called in friendly artillery exterminators to blast the snipers out. But when you came right down to it, when we were already in the rubble, it became sniper against sniper.

Dog-tired and footsore, my company on point for the battalion wended its way into one of those count-less, nameless towns we encountered on the way to Rome. It had been gutted by shellfire; the point men blazed a pathway around piles of brick and collapsed frameworks and broken glass. My squad was holding down a place with the headquarters element toward the rear of the formation when a shot echoed ahead in the ruins. From where I was, all I could see was the backs of GIs as they ducked behind parts of walls and buildings, crouching there and not moving. The com-pany commander went scurrying to the front, followed by his radio man. I always looked for that antenna when I was deciding which enemy to shoot.

A few minutes later, I heard another shot. And another. I figured it for a sniper, but I held my men tight until a runner came sliding in next to me. He was panting with excitement.

"The old man wants snipers. That fucking kraut's got three of us drilled up there already."

I tapped the sniper next to me for a spotter. The runner stayed behind with his head down while my spotter and I dodged forward from building to building until we reached the commander crouching behind the remains of a house. He was breathing heavily, and sweat had matted plaster dust on his face until he resembled a mime.

"We don't know where the hell the bastard is out there," the CO said.

I had to chance a look. I crawled to the end of the building. I had learned to memorize every detail of terrain after one quick peek. I took that peek from right next to the ground, past some kind of bottle half-filled with spoiled food.

To my front was a street that ran away from me to where it intersected another street filled with debris from a recent shelling. A bed with the mattress still on it rested atop a pile of concrete wreckage. One of the dead GIs lay at the intersection. He seemed so much a part of the general waste that you hardly noticed him. By his position, I figured the sniper's hide to be farther down the street where he could control both it and the intersection.

"Keep everybody down and in position," I instructed the CO. "Give us a little while. We'll see if we can take care of him."

My spotter and I worked our way from point to point. The hiding GIs watched as we cut across an alley blind to the sniper's street and eased cautiously along a shell-pocked wall overgrown with dead ivy. The wall bisected a little knoll coming off what once must have been someone's front yard. From there we had a long view up the street. We settled down to look things over. Being a sniper required patience.

"Krauts don't watch Roy Rogers," I whispered to my partner. "Let's give him a target and see if he shows himself."

We had used the trick before. My spotter crawled down to the end of the wall nearest the street while I eased my M-1 through a crack clogged with enough ivy to camouflage my movements. As I watched the terrain through my scope, my spotter put his helmet on a stick and slowly thrust it above the wall. He jerked it back down and waited a minute or two before revealing it again. This time the sniper was ready. Krauts *didn't* watch Roy Rogers or they would have recognized the oldest sagebrush trick in the Old West.

An 8-millimeter German bullet drilled the helmet and sent it spinning.

I caught movement through my scope. A thin puff of smoke popped from the window of a building about a hundred yards down the street. There wasn't much left of the building, but it still had enough roof over its remaining window to hold shadows inside.

I held my fire. It was like when you spooked a squirrel into its hole. All you had to do was sit down and wait. Sooner or later curiosity overcame caution and the squirrel stuck its head out again. I kept my scope centered on the window, waiting. A good sniper, a survivor, never shot more than two or three times from the same hide. I was counting on this German being careless or lazy.

The day was overcast and it was dark inside the house behind the glassless window. Presently, however, I detected a slight movement. I shifted my cross hairs slightly and bided my time. Hunting animals gives you the patience to hunt man. Soon, I picked up the dull momentary gleam of a rifle barrel. Then a faint outline materialized as the kraut peeked out to see what was going on. Just like a squirrel.

I fired.

An invisible rope yanked the German's weapon from his hands and hurled it into the street. The German's body lunged forward across the window sill where it hung head down, his hands fluttering a moment against the street. The body spasmed a few more times and drained a dark pool of blood below its head. Then it was still.

I was scalping the dead German when a green lieutenant who had just hooked up with the outfit came up to see what was happening.

"Omigod!"

He turned to the paleness of a west Texas sky in the middle of summer.

"You barbarian sonofabitch! Whattaya think you're doing?"

He was turning from pale to a mesquite gray green. I grinned and held up the fresh scalp. It was still dripping.

"Whatsa matter, sir? Ain't you never seen a dead kraut before?"

He made it behind a wall before he started puking.

"Guess he ain't at that."

CHAPTER FOUR

U.S. Army Sergeant
William E. Jones
Normandy, 1944

On the range at Fort Dix I fired the highest score of any enlisted man in I Company, Eighth Infantry Regiment, Fourth Division. Because of that and because of no other reason that I know of, I got volunteered to be the company sniper. We only had one for each company. My platoon sergeant sent me down to the armorer who signed me out a factory-new, bolt-action .30-caliber 1903 Springfield with the finest scope—one of the *only* scopes—this ol' son of an Appalachian sharecropper ever saw.

The armorer grinned.

"It ain't a woman, Jones. Don't stroke it."

"I ain't never seen a rifle as purty as this one."

"Well, you take that rifle, Jones. It'll kill some Germans for you when you get over there if you'll take care of it."

Everyone else in the company had either the standard issue M-1 Garand or the shorter .30-caliber carbine. Because of *the rifle,* everybody knew who I was. I was *the sniper.* That was how I thought of that relationship too—*the rifle; the sniper.*

Because we were hill people when I was growing up and had to depend on eating squirrels and rabbits and 'possums to survive, I had become a fair shot with a .22. I got even better with *the rifle.* After I got it zeroed in just right, I could hit anything I wanted. I knew what elevation I needed for a certain range and I could find it by the clicks on the scope, day or night. I might have been slower than the other boys with their Garands, but I knew I was a great deal more accurate. I could hit what I shot at.

My job was to shoot folks 'way out there. I heard some of the other divisions had sniper schools to learn that, but I guess the brass didn't think I needed any schooling, the way I could shoot already.

The Fourth Division hit Utah Beach at Normandy on June 6, 1944. We didn't draw much resistance on our part of the beach, but I heard there was hell to pay farther down where the boys were dying in the water. Still, it was no place for a country boy to be. Within hours, we were off the sand, and from then on my company acted as the spearhead for the regiment. We started moving forward, gaining real estate, through the damnedest country I ever saw. If Tennessee was God's country, then this country, being opposite Tennessee on the other side of the world, had to have been Hell. The French called it *bocage,* something like that, but the dogfaces called it lots of names other than what it really was. History was to call it simply the hedgerows.

The countryside was a patchwork quilt of little fields enclosed by hedges of hawthorn, brambles, and vines tangled together to make walls ten to fifteen feet tall. A lot of the hedges grew out of big mounds three to four feet high, with drainage ditches on either side. They grew out over the roads, which were nothing but wagon trails with deep ruts in them, and made it seem like you were going down through a tunnel. When it rained—and it rained a lot—mud caked on your boots, vehicles were always getting stuck and having to be pushed out by tanks, and all you could see in front of you was gloom and the dripping, shaggy walls of the hedgerows.

One dogface slogged around a bend in the tunnel road and surprised a jerry hiding in the hedges. They were staring at each other almost eyeball to eyeball. They could have reached out and touched one another. Neither one of them thought to shoot.

The GI yelled: "Shoo! Get the hell outa here!" And the German took off.

The hedgerows on their mounds turned each little vineyard or cornfield into a fort. Germans dug in and you almost had to burn them out. If their artillery spotters saw us, then we expected a shelling. You heard a machine gun rattling someplace up ahead or over on one flank and you felt sorry for the poor bastards who were getting that, but you were thankful *they* were getting it instead of *you*. There was firing someplace all the time, but you never saw anything unless it was right around and on you. You tramped on up through the rain around a bend in the road and across some field and through the hedges where a tank had gone first with those big knives on it and ripped a way through. You maybe saw a dead GI or two lying there in the mud that graves registration hadn't got to yet. You looked at them with their blood seeping out and mixing with the rain. Sometimes you knew them, but you kept on going anyhow.

You fought from field to field and crawled and slopped through pelting rain and ankle-deep mud. The sick-sweet stink of death seeped into everything. If it wasn't dead Germans and sometimes a dead GI, then it was dead cows all bloated up or a horse or goat or something that got caught by artillery or in a crossfire. I must have seen five hundred dead cows.

Sometimes you discovered a fresh shallow grave topped with a wooden cross or a boltless rifle stuck muzzle-down into the mud with a helmet on top of it. I don't know how many folks died in the hedgerow fighting after D-day, but there had to have been a lot of them. We just kept going and kept going. It was the same thing day after day. Mostly we didn't know where we were going and some of us forgot where we started from. They just told you to go up that road or across that field and you went. War in the hedgerows came down to just what you could see from one hedge to another.

It was country tailor-made for ambushes and snipers. The lanes were death traps as much for tanks as for dogfaces. The Germans had machine guns and snipers mounted on wooden platforms in the trees. The snipers used flashless gunpowder. That made it hard to spot them. They kept picking us off. It got to where you suspected danger in every blade of grass. You dreaded the next bend in the road. It got where you had almost rather be shot on the spot and put out of your misery than have to go around another bend or across another field and face another machine gun or another sniper picking you and your buddies off one by one.

I kept *the rifle* spotless and rust free for whenever some German sniper pinned us down and the call came back for ol' Bill Jones to come up front with *the rifle* and spot the German and get rid of him. *The rifle* was some piece of smooth machinery. In my pack among C-rats and old moldy socks and underwear that was supposed to be dry but wasn't, I kept a little can of oil, a cleaning rod, and some bore patches. Steel rusted in that climate overnight. Without oil, the chamber of an M-1 would rust tight within a week. I fought the rust constantly. No matter how beat I was, or scared, or anything else, every time I got the chance I ran my hand down the barrel of that '03 Springfield and if there was a rough place I broke out my cleaning gear and attacked the rust before it got a good start. Whenever I could, I disassembled the parts on a spread-out poncho and looked down the bore and felt in the chamber for rust and carbon. I would have liked some wax for the stock, as it took a beating in the hedges, but I didn't have any, so I oiled it down using an old sock.

With the telescopic sight, I could often find the German snipers hiding in the hedgerows. You couldn't see them with the naked eye, but the 10X scope brought them right out of hiding. When I was needed I crawled up to where I could see, generally from one hedgerow across a field to another hedgerow, and started scanning. After I found him, it was easier than shooting a squirrel. Give me the tip of a squirrel's nose in a cottonwood and I could shoot it off with a .22; give me a piece of helmet or a part of a face or shoulder at 300 or 400 yards, which was a long shot in that type of terrain, and I could nip it off with the Springfield.

I could always tell when I was needed. There would be a single shot, followed by "Medic! Medic!"

When the call came back, I wriggled on my belly up through the roots and brambles, careful to keep *the rifle* out of the mud and not bang the scope out of adjustment. I remember one day when the sun was shining for a change, and it reminded me of a good spring day back in the Smoky Mountains. Except those weren't geese flying back north overhead, they were artillery shells. The singing you heard wasn't a meadowlark, it was a German machine gun. And that was no hammerhead woodpecker tapping, it was bullets hitting trees.

I slithered down a little gully and worked my way up to another sergeant lying in a depression with his helmet off and the sun shining on red hair. He looked at me and gave a thin smile, then looked back across an open field of short new grass that abutted a hedgerow about three hundred yards away. A low hill rose beyond it, on top of which perched an old farmhouse. The empty windows did not reflect the sunlight; the panes were gone, shot out probably.

I kept my head low while I started to scan the hedgerows through my scope. The German sniper was no slouch. He had already picked off two of our boys. I heard a medic over in the bushes working on one of them.

"Lung," the red-headed sergeant muttered.

"What?"

"The kraut got his lung. You know how it's all pink and bubbly when they get a lung?"

"Yeah."

"You got the bastard spotted yet?"

Trees grew thick out of the hedgerow. They were all bushed out this time of year. It's hard to see squirrels after the spring budding.

"Not yet," I said.

"I think it might have come from over to the right."

I detected a large dark knot high in the top of a tree. I studied it a second and was about to slide on past, thinking it a deformity in the tree, when it moved. I watched it intently, finally concluding that I must have seen a bird, although most of the birds had left. I scoped slowly on down the hedgerow, hoping the sniper would reveal himself.

When nothing else stirred, I returned to the knot for lack of anything more probable. The more I looked at it, the more it resembled a man hugged tight to the tree trunk. The redheaded sergeant cleared his throat.

"It's either him," I replied, "or a knot in a tree."

"Shoot it and see what happens."

"I'll wait."

I didn't want the sniper spotting me first if that really was a knot. I studied the length of the hedgerows again before returning to the tree. Several minutes passed. The sergeant fidgeted.

"I want him to break first," I explained.

The next time the knot moved, I knew it was not a bird.

"Okay, I have him!" I said triumphantly.

A slight breeze drifted across the field from left to right, stirring with its breath a few pale spears of grass. I clicked in a degree of windage and clicked one up on elevation. The workings were smooth. I kept them that way. The good sun provided me a sharp picture through the scope, although the foliage concealed most of what I at first mistook to be a "knot."

The sucker had shot at least two of our boys. With that in mind and nothing else, I drew in a deep breath filled with the smell of the rich soil on which I lay, let half of it slowly escape, and then gentle stroked the trigger. *The rifle* recoiled.

When I brought it back down, I saw the tree shaking violently. The "knot" seemed to be throbbing and pulsating. I quickly bolted in another round and put my cross hairs back on target. Sometimes you had to hit a squirrel two or three times when it was high in the reaches of some sycamore or cottonwood and all you could get the first time was a piece of him.

I squeezed off another round. The German turned loose his perch just like a squirrel does and bounced off the limbs down through the tree until his body hit the ground.

The redheaded sergeant pounded me on the back.

"That murderin' sonuvabitch!" he shouted. "You got him."

I glanced at the corpse as the company got back in battle formation and straggled across the field and by him. I glanced at him and didn't want to look any harder, but I did. He was just a kid with sandy hair in dirty gray green. His helmet lay beside him. My first bullet must have made the bloody gash across his ribs. The second popped open his chest. His eyes were slitted apart and without luster. His teeth shone dully between his lips. A squirrel's teeth always shone like that when you shot it.

"Pay-back time," the sergeant said cheerily. "You got him in the heart. He was dead before he hit the ground."

That was my only "confirmed" kill, if "confirmed" meant you had to go up and look at his teeth shining between his lips and pick out the bullet hole. Most of the time when I zapped one, the other Germans either dragged him off or we were too fagged out to worry about going up to take a look at where he fell. All dead men looked the same anyhow. They smelled the same too. After they lay around in the sun and rain for a few days and bloated up and split open, you couldn't tell a German corpse from a GI by the smell. For that matter, you couldn't tell the smell from a dead cow either.

Every time we ran across tankers, they were complaining that they couldn't see more than a foot or two in any direction. The hedgerows weren't meant for tanks. If the tankers unbuttoned and stuck their heads out, they were asking for a sniper round. If they remained buttoned, they were blind in the gloomy tunnels and the Germans got them with *panzerfaust* rockets.

"Fuck you tankers," I overheard a dispirited dogface growl at a tanker. "You fuckers oughta be out here *walking* in this shit where you don't even have your iron boxes to hide in."

"Fuck you," snapped the tanker.

"Fuck *you*," said the dogface.

I felt like I was a match for the Germans as long as I had *the rifle* and kept it functioning. Snipers didn't walk point like the rest of the grunts. I stayed back with headquarters and only went to work when we got pinned down. You eased down those narrow soggy roads surrounded by hedges, and the tension left you feeling like a wet rag. My heart would skip like a flat rock across a pond every time a single shot rang out. A machine gun was something else, or an ambush. But the single shot meant I generally went to work. The spotlight was on me. Everybody else got down and watched from the sidelines.

It was better than walking point or assaulting machine guns. I slipped up, found the squirrel wherever he was hiding, and shot him. That was it. Somebody said, "Good shooting, Jonesy." Somebody else would look out toward where the jerry fell and mutter something like, "Cocksucking Nazi motherfucker." Then the GIs would start slowly moving again and I would drop back to wait until the next time. While the other GIs were targets for German snipers, the German snipers were *my* targets.

The strain of the hedgerows wore on you. It felt like we had fought all the way across France and should be damned near to Germany. We just kept going until the next machine gun ambush or next sniper or the next time the Germans shelled us. We fell face down in the mud right where we were. I cursed the Germans for that, and for making me get *the rifle* muddy.

Each night a lieutenant or sergeant checked off the names of the day's wounded and dead. They had been your buddies, but the fatigue had got to you so that it was no more than someone glumly reading names out of the Nashville telephone directory. If there was a world outside these hedgerows, none of us expected to see it again. My mind was so dulled by it all that I couldn't even remember Tennessee sometimes.

We came to some open fields. The sun hung low in the west and reflected red shimmering balls in the puddles of rain-filled shell craters ahead of us. I took a deep breath. It felt good to draw in air untainted by the moldy hedgerows. As we started digging in for the night behind the camouflage of a weed-choked fence, I leaned *the rifle* against a stunted persimmon, the only tree anywhere about.

I hadn't much more than started my foxhole before the Germans spotted us and rained down mortar shells on us. I threw myself into what shallow excavation I had and rammed my hands up inside my helmet and grabbed the straps to hold the helmet on and maybe keep shrapnel from whacking off my hands. I held on in desperation while the ground shook like a drenched dog, explosions went flash-bang in a weird dance of death around and through us, and hot chunks of metal zipped and whirred overhead. The shelling chewed up the ground and the fence line like a bunch of giant gophers with steel jaws. I heard men screaming and moaning. Tomorrow, some French farmer would be mending fence and a glum lieutenant would be reading some more names from the telephone directory.

After an eternity that lasted from Columbus to Franklin Roosevelt's first election, the mortars stopped. The earth settled. Medics started treating the wounded. I opened one eye and looked around. When nothing happened, I opened the other eye.

The first thing my eyes settled on was the persimmon tree where I left *the rifle*. It looked like Charles Atlas had grabbed the tree and twisted it off just above the ground. I didn't see *the rifle*.

I jumped up and made a frenzied dash to the tree stump. All I could do was stand there and stare like I'd lost my best buddy. I kept that weapon cleaned and oiled to do a job when I needed it—and now it was just pieces of useless scrap metal scattered all over the countryside.

I could have cried.

The next night when the gloomy lieutenant checked off the names of the dead and wounded, I didn't say anything about *the rifle,* but I mentally added it to the list. *The rifle.* After it was gone I was just another dogface GI with an M-1 Garand in the hedgerows.

CHAPTER FIVE

When Lieutenant Claude N. Harris told his student snipers at Green's Farm that snipers could save a country, he always used Russia as an example. While Russian partisans lacked the strength to engage in open battle with the German invaders, they still proved such a threat to the *Wehrmacht* with their ever present banging from the trees and their hit-and-run tactics that the Germans issued a warning to their troops:

"We Germans make the mistake of thinking that if neither offensive nor defensive operations are in progress then there is no war at all. But the war is going on . . . when we are cooking potatoes, when we lie down to sleep. A soldier must carry his weapon always and everywhere."

The ability to carry the war to the enemy and strike like a scalpel flicking off pieces of the enemy's flesh, bringing him terror and uncertainty, slowing him down and even stalling him indefinitely with a relatively few skilled riflemen—that remains the strength of the intensely individual and rather lonely art of the sniper.

Brought into its own by the technology of accurate long-range weapons and by skills developed by men like Captain Herbert W. McBride and others before and after him, the art and the science of the sniper has been well utilized by soldiers on all continents. Marksmen have, as Lieutenant Harris liked to point out, literally saved their countries on many occasions.

During Napoleon's peninsular campaigns from 1808–14, Spanish guerrillas used snipers to cut and harass the lines of supply and communications leading from France to battle zones in Spain. Firing weapons like the .653-caliber Baker with a flintlock firing device that a modern expert would reject with hoots of derision, the Spanish snipers included scores of men among them whose aim, patience, and powers of concealment ranked them with Sergeant Carlos Hathcock, Captain McBride, or any other sniper in history. Perched in the highlands overlooking the highways along which supply convoys had to make their way, blending into their tawny backgrounds, the Spanish sharpshooters held Napoleon's French entirely at their mercy.

A hillside apparently sleeping in the sun suddenly puffed a little spot of blue gun smoke and a blue-clad transport driver toppled into the dust before the report of the gunshot reached him. When the escort swung to blaze away in the direction of the shot, a second Spanish rifle cracked from a different vantage point and another shako rolled heavily across the ruts. Then the sniper disappeared, only to reappear at the next bend in the road.

Faced with a mounting toll of slaughtered French service troops and muleteers, Napoleon had to withdraw more and more combat troops to protect his convoys. When that proved no defense and the reign of terror continued, the French built strongholds and small forts every few kilometers along the road between which the frightened *camioneers* scurried like mice from one hole to the next. Strengthening the escorts, doubling up on the size of the convoys, stationing security in the hills and at the bends of the road—none of it discouraged the Spanish snipers. Menace still lurked behind every lonely crag or withered pine. The single, well-aimed shot continued to take its toll. As an old Spanish proverb put it: "What cares the wolf how many sheep there be?"

Europe's twenty-year struggle with Napoleon yielded one other remarkable, if unorthodox, example of sniping.

On the morning of October 21, 1805, Private Robert Guillemard, on service with the French fleet, rode high in the fighting top of the *Redoubtable* as the English fleet bore down upon the combined Franco-Spanish armament. Peering through the drifting cannon smoke, Guillemard made out the figure of a man in an admiral's jacket whose breast was covered with bright battle decorations. Taking careful aim as the *Redoubtable* rode easy on a gentle swell, the Frenchman pressed his trigger. Thus it was that in the hour of its greatest triumph, England's most famous admiral, Lord Horatio Nelson, fell victim to the sniper's deadly art.

Men such as these have shot their way into history, men who could lie patiently hidden behind a parapet or who could wait as John Unertl once did in World War I for three days, defecating in his pants to keep from moving, in order to get a single accurate shot. They have surrounded themselves with an aura of mystery and awe that has magnified tales about them into the stuff of legend. It is with respect that today's

British soldier still speaks of "Jim The Nailer" from the time of the Indian Mutiny.

During the siege of the Lucknow Residency, a garrison of 1,700, of whom no more than one-half were Europeans, found themselves surrounded and besieged by Indians in revolt against Her Majesty's government. While the defenders used their skills of marksmanship against the Indians to save ammunition and keep the rebels at bay, there was one wily marksman beyond the breastworks and outer walls whose skills with a rifle outmatched any of the defenders. Having chosen his hide with infinite care, he waited with an unblinking patience that the hot noon sun or the chill of night could not daunt. Remaining unseen and inactive for hours at a stretch, he swung into action only at the flash of a scarlet tunic or white cap cover. His unerring gunfire took account with such deadly precision that the sweating men of the garrison paid tribute by dubbing him "Jim The Nailer."

His exact "body count" is as impossible to compute as is his specific identity. After the British broke the siege, he vanished into legend as Jim The Nailer, a sniper as imperishable as the story of the Lucknow siege itself.

If the art of sniping is composed of guile and patience and marksmanship, perhaps none better demonstrated these qualities of the sniper than did young Ensign Baron Steinfurst-Wallenstein during the Franco-German campaign of 1870–71.

The Germans' breech-loading "needle" guns were outranged by the French *chassepot*, which was used with deadly effectiveness as the lines closed in around beleaguered Paris. Snipers from the Gallic outposts popped continuously at the forward German outposts. Particularly victimized were Germans on the eastern outskirts of the capital where a French marksman occupied an upper room in a gardener's cottage. Shooting from such a range that the Germans could not possibly return effective fire, this Frenchman systematically plucked off man after man until the young cavalry officer named Steinfurst-Wallenstein offered to stalk the enemy sniper. An expert gameshot, he thought his own favorite rifle might be able to even the score.

Before first light, he slipped silently through his lines' snowbound outposts and burrowed into a clump of evergreens at an angle from the gardener's cottage. When the gray morning dawned, the sniper's window gaped back at him with a black and glassless eye. It was not until the winter's sun slowly burned off the morning haze that the ensign detected a whisper of movement at the back of the room. The French marksman was keeping watch on the German outposts from the shadows. He never approached the window itself.

Three times during the day the flash of a gunshot flickered from the room's shadows. The German peered eagerly down his sights, hoping for a glimpse of the man who kept himself so carefully hidden. Once more he caught a hint of movement, but he held his fire. He realized he was unlikely to get a second shot if his first missed.

At dusk, stiff from cold but not discouraged, the little baron stole back to his own lines, determined to continue his vigil come another dawn. One dead man and two wounded at battalion headquarters told of the French sniper's deadly activities. But the baron knew that sooner or later the Frenchman would relax.

After the second evening of the baron's stalk ended, and the young officer came slipping back to his lines after dark, his battalion commander sternly ordered him to return to his regular duties. The French sniper had killed another German during the day.

"Zu befehl, Herr Major," responded the young officer with a slight smile. "But when it is light enough in the morning for you to use your field glasses, I think you will find that my time has not been wasted."

The incredulous battalion commander stood at first light to focus his binoculars on the cottage. To his amazement, he saw the Frenchman's body hanging head down from the gaping window. As Steinfurst-Wallenstein explained it, the Frenchman had, as always, aimed and fired from the back of the room. However, he finally made the mistake for which the baron had been waiting. On his last shot of the previous day, he stepped to the window to check the effect of his marksmanship. That was when the baron's patience paid off in the failing light.

At the outset of World War I, the Germans were so prepared for trench warfare and the siege conditions of sniping and counter-sniping that accompanied it that by the end of the first year of the war they were employing no less than 20,000 rifles fitted with telescopic sights. Having up to 6 sniper's rifles per company, the Germans for a time dominated the front lines.

But if the Germans possess a genius for organization, the British faculty for improvisation under the inspiration of a few real shooting enthusiasts, among them the American Captain Herbert W. McBride, soon established sniper schools and worked out an operational modus operandi that set the pattern for snipers in both World Wars, in Korea, and in Vietnam. These principles are still taught today at the U.S. Marine Corps and U.S. Army sniper schools. The art of the sniper combined with the technology of science to make the single well-aimed shot the most deadly weapon on the battlefield.

Nowhere was this better illustrated than in the ruins

of Stalingrad during World War II when Russian snipers stopped the advance of a superior Nazi force in action that proved to be the turning point of the war on the eastern front. Stalingrad saw some of the most intense sniper activity in history.

Following days of siege and heavy bombardment that destroyed much of the city, the German Sixth Army and the Fourth Panzer Army began entering downtown Stalingrad on September 14, 1942. Russian marksmen armed with Moisan Nagant 7.62 bolt-action sniper rifles riddled the *Wehrmacht* ranks as the Germans picked their way through the ruins. The Germans had to overcome each sniper nest as they came to it, at a cost of time and men that permitted the Red Army to bring up light artillery and militia "storm groups."

Training for the Russian snipers lasted two days before, pressed for time, the graduates were hurled into battle. The school operated from the Lazur Chemical Plant, a huge building that remained in Russian hands. Instructors painted outlines of soldiers and helmets on a wall and hovered over the trainees to help them nail down basic sniper techniques.

War correspondents soon made famous the name of a young hunter from the Ural Mountains who was credited with forty-two kills during one ten-day period. When news of Vassili Zaitsev's feats reached German headquarters, the German staff became obsessed with destroying Zaitsev as an example to others and as a boost to their harried soldiers' courage. The Germans had grown weary of the devastating effects of the Russian snipers on their troops' lives and morale.

In what must be the most remarkable example of champions facing off against each other since the days of the Roman gladiators or the European knights, Germany shipped its own hero to Stalingrad to hunt down Zaitsev. Although each army was preparing for a final pitched battle in the city ruins, the lines went static and held breathlessly when it became clear that the two marksmen were meeting in a personal duel in the no-man's-land between lines—the champion of the Red Army against the hero of the *Wehrmacht* in a life-or-death struggle from which only one must emerge.

The German sniper, a major named Konings, pored over every newspaper article and document he could find about Zaitsev. Zaitsev, on the other hand, had learned well the tactics and patterns of German snipers in general, but had no way of knowing Konings' personal style. He knew only that Konings had apparently headed a German sniper school in Berlin.

Konings started the duel. He crept into the rubble of Stalingrad and killed two Soviet snipers, each with a single shot. That was the challenge. Konings had announced his presence and established the battle site.

Zaitsev and his spotter Nikolai Kulikov scanned the front between Mamaev Hill and the Red October Plant. The lines here had gone static to await the outcome of the sniper encounter. The artillery fire and bombing in the distance faded out of the Russians' minds as they concentrated. They noted every terrain feature in front of them, committing everything to memory—the streets strewn with toppled buildings, the still-standing walls of other buildings, broken power poles, the burned skeletons of both military and civilian vehicles. A sniper had a thousand places to hide. Zaitsev knew, as did Konings out there in the rubble, that the war for them narrowed down to a single shot.

The first day passed without either sniper showing himself, although, toward evening when the shadows were stretching long and ragged across the battlefield, Zaitsev spotted a German helmet as its owner peeped across the contested ground. The Russian saved his shot. It could be a trick to make him reveal his position.

When night fell, the sniper on each side cautiously withdrew to his own lines.

"My guts tell me he is out there watching and waiting," Zaitsev commented to his spotter. "He will return tomorrow."

Before dawn the next day, Zaitsev and Kulikov burrowed into the wreckage of a bombed building, while Konings the challenger made his nest underneath a discarded scrap of steel surrounded by rubble. He peered through a small space. He waited. Zaitsev and Kulikov waited. The battle of nerves, patience, and wit continued through the second day as it had the first.

On the third day, a political officer named Danilov accompanied the Russians to their hide. He wanted to see the fight for himself. Zaitsev protested, but Danilov, of course, had his way. When the sun rose, Danilov, squinting across the shattered landscape, thought he saw something move. Overcome by his excitement, he sprang to his knees, pointing.

"There he is! There he is! I'll point him out to you!"

Konings knew such behavior did not mark the calculated behavior of his rival. Hoping it would make Zaitsev reveal himself in order to help a wounded comrade, Konings deliberately drilled the gesticulating Russian through the shoulder. Danilov went down hard, screaming and writhing in fright and pain. Zaitsev did not stir; he was too wily for that. He remained in his hide, using his binoculars in an effort to locate the origin of the gunshot.

Konings did not fire again either, even when stretcher bearers came scuttling forward through the battle debris to roll Danilov onto a stretcher and hurriedly tote him to the rear.

Zaitsev thought he had narrowed down the German's hide to somewhere between a burned-out tank on his left front and a destroyed pillbox on the right. It was that area between littered with piles of destruction that Zaitsev carefully studied through binoculars. Of particular interest was a slab of steel fallen at the corner of a building and then covered with rubbish. He focused on a dark spot beneath the metal. It appeared to be a hollow underneath the steel and wreckage, an excellent sniper's nest.

Knowing Danilov had given away the location of his hide and that Konings would be expecting him to try to change his location, Zaitsev suspected the German would be prepared to fire at whatever moved. He slid a stick into a glove and slowly thrust it above his head. Sure enough, Konings's rifle cracked and the glove jerked.

"That's our viper," Zaitsev said.

He cautiously wriggled backwards out of his hide, followed by Kulikov, and the pair of Russians used most of the day low-crawling inch by inch to another hide. The sun was going down by the time the Russians selected their new positions, with Kulikov hiding some distance away on Zaitsev's right flank. The sun glared through the torn city behind the German and directly into Zaitsev's eyes. Konings waited, watching. He had the advantage if Zaitsev chose to continue the exchange.

Zaitsev chose to wait for the sun to come up behind *his* back and into the German's eyes. It was a cold, long night for both snipers. Neither dared give up an inch for fear of yielding the advantage to the other. It became the deadliest chess match of all.

On the fourth morning, while the opposing German and Russian lines waited on the outcome, Zaitsev initiated the first step of his plan. Kulikov fired a single shot to deliberately give away his position. Zaitsev hoped the German would think the Russian's nerves had broken and that he had shot at a shadow. Then Zaitsev waited for the sun to climb directly into Konings's eyes before he brought out step two.

Kulikov slowly lifted his helmet on a stick while Zaitsev centered his scope directly on the dark spot beneath the mangled steel in the rubble of no-man's-land where he suspected the German hid. The long ordeal must also be weighing heavily upon Konings's nerves. He must also be wanting to have this duel over and done with.

Zaitsev picked up a glinted reflection from a scope as the German instantly shot Kulikov's helmet, sending it flying. Kulikov emitted a bloodcurdling scream of pain and thrashed about to further distract the German sniper. Satisfied that he had his man, Zaitsev aimed and squeezed off his only shot in four days. The bullet blasted through Konings's face and out the back of his helmet.

Vassili Zaitsev remained champion in the only modern duel between sharpshooters for which outcome entire armies waited. Before the Battle of Stalingrad ended, Zaitsev racked up a body count in excess of 140 Germans and was awarded the Order of Lenin.

Japanese soldiers in the Pacific campaigns, in their efforts to delay and stall the American island-hopping advance, employed sniper tactics similar to those the Soviets used against the Nazis. Equipped with hooks on their boots for climbing trees, Japanese suicide squads perched hidden in the jungle foliage and pinned down enemy patrols for hours and even days. Others forted up in deep caves in the hills back of the shorelines and poured sniper and machine gun fire onto approaching Marines until they were rooted out with flame throwers or killed by high-explosive charges.

Americans learned to dread sniper fire more than they feared the direct encounter of a human-wave attack.

An officer who was showing General Douglas MacArthur around after the Marines landed on Los Negros in the Admiralties tried to steer him away from a patch of jungle near the beachhead.

"We killed a Jap sniper in there just a few minutes ago," he explained.

"Fine," MacArthur replied. "That's the best thing to do with them."

Although American snipers were trained at such places as Green's Farm and at dozens of other impromptu schools springing up from Hawaii to the Solomons, they found few opportunities to engage in classic sniper warfare such as that in Europe where Allied marksmen exchanged terror for terror in the bloody sniper wars. Snipers are best utilized on the defensive, as the Japanese and Russians knew, or on a slow-moving or static battlefield. When combat tactics call for fast-moving assaults in force, it is difficult and impractical to station sniper teams to wait for the odd enemy soldier or patrol to present itself. American scout snipers in the Pacific were primarily used therefore to root out machine guns and enemy snipers. Their casualties ran high.

"Mac, I'll see you someday, but not on this earth," sniper William Deane "Hawk" Hawkins told a friend before he shipped out to the Pacific.

After winning a battlefield commission to first lieutenant at Guadalcanal, Hawkins was assigned command of a scout/sniper platoon. His mission on Betio was to lead his platoon in ahead of the first invasion waves and clear the long pier of Japanese snipers and machine gunners. Although it was the toughest assignment of the morning, his men quickly completed the mission by using grenades, flame throwers, and accurate rifle fire.

Then Hawk led his men over the sea wall and stayed ahead of the battle most of the day, sniping Japanese snipers, blasting out entrenched positions, returning to the rear only to get more ammunition.

"He's a madman!" exclaimed a fellow officer who saw him riding back to the front on an amtrac. "Running around with a million bullets a minute whistling by his ears, just shooting Japs."

Someone yelled at him to get down.

"Aw, those bastards can't shoot!" he yelled back. "They can't hit anything."

Hawk stood in full view to shoot point blank through pillbox firing slits and to toss in grenades while his men laid down cover fire. A mortar shell killed three of his men and wounded him, but he kept fighting.

"I came here to kill Japs, not to be evacuated," he snapped at a corpsman who tried to hold him back.

He blew up three more pillboxes after being wounded. One of his sergeants later described what happened after that:

"We were attacking a sort of fort at the base of a sandy knoll. Hawk started tossing grenades from close up. He had got rid of maybe half a dozen when a heavy machine gun opened up and an explosive shell hit him in the shoulder. The blood just gushed out of him."

Hawkins received the Medal of Honor posthumously. The Betio airstrip was later renamed Hawkins Field in honor of the sniper who came "to kill Japs."

CHAPTER SIX

U.S. Marine Private
Daniel Webster Cass, Jr.
Okinawa, 1945

We were going to make the landing on Easter morning. Some of the guys were talking the night before in the belly of the transport that was taking us in for the landing. They were talking about what they used to do back home on Easter Sunday. One of them chuckled, remembering, but the chuckling stopped before it really started. I got up off my bunk and went somewhere else so I wouldn't have to listen to them. I didn't feel like talking. I kept feeling like I was going to be sick.

The old hands who had fought ashore at such places as Guadalcanal or Peleliu got real silent too, or else they got talkative to keep from listening to their guts roll around inside. The rest of us, the green ones, banged the chained bunks down from the bulkheads and crawled into them fully clothed. There was almost none of the usual grab-assing. Somebody told me that the night before the first one was always the worst and that the *anticipation* of combat was worse than the combat itself. I couldn't believe that. We smelled each other's sweat and fear and heard silences inside ourselves that even listening to the talkative ones could not dispel.

When you couldn't sleep, you got up and got into a high-stakes poker game on a blanket spread on the deck or on somebody's bunk. You cleaned your bayonet and your ammo. You repacked mess gear, clean socks and underwear, shaving gear, field rations, a picture of your wife or sweetheart. The holds of the ships were so crowded you could hardly squeeze through them. You saw a Bible lying on a bunk here, there an unfinished paperback book or a pack of letters home. You bitched about it all. About the weather, the food, the war, each other. It took your mind off tomorrow.

The ones who had not turned introspective spoke in low quick tones of the First Marines at places like Old Baldy and Bloody Nose Ridge and Five Sisters. The eyes of one of the vets who was cleaning his M-1 crawled deep into their sockets. They glinted faintly like a dying fire inside a cave.

"After Peleliu," he said slowly, "there wasn't no more First Marines. It was another Tarawa. I hear eight guys are getting the Medal of Honor posthumously. Maybe it was nine."

"Posthumously?"

"Dead. Along with about three thousand other Marines from the First Division."

Somebody else said, hopefully, "They didn't hit us on the beaches at Iwo Jima."

"They'll hit us on the beaches here though. Did you see the way them hills come right down to the water? We'll be setting ducks. This'll be *worse* than Tarawa."

I broke out my '03 Springfield and oiled it down with a cloth. It didn't need it, but it gave me something to do. I cleaned the 10X scope and made sure the "traveling" mount slid smoothly. I did it automatically. I must have done it a hundred times before, a thousand times, since I learned we were sailing to Okinawa. I peered through the scope to make sure not even a speck of dust fouled it.

I glanced up as Corporal Chester Carter slid onto the bunk next to me. He didn't say anything for awhile, but the lean Texas face beneath the sandy hair skinned tight to the sides of his head Marine boot-style seemed even leaner than normal. A sniper and a spotter worked as a team. Carter was my spotter. We had trained together at a sniper school on a cattle farm back at Camp Pendleton. I kept wiping down my rifle, trying to look casual. He was trying just as hard not to look scared. At nineteen years old, I was younger than him by a year or two and a half-head taller. I didn't say anything because I wasn't sure I could control the tremor in my voice.

Finally, Carter spoke.

"No more cow shit and yellow chalk," he said with an effort at nonchalance.

My grin felt wooden. For six weeks in California and in the Russell Islands we had undergone training in scouting, map reading, compass, and the like. During practice exercises we hid in the dark and marked the other Marines with yellow chalk when they passed to show a "kill." One night we bombarded an officers' bivouac with handfuls of cow shit.

It was the real thing now though.

"No more cow shit and yellow chalk," I agreed.

A grunt paused to watch me with the rifle. He had the hollow eyes and sunken cheeks of a veteran. He looked at our boot camp haircuts.

"You guys ever done any of this sniping before?" he asked.

"This is our first time," I admitted.

He looked at us again. Then he shook his head, said, "Good luck," and walked off.

Carter sounded alarmed: "What does he mean by that?—good luck."

"Just . . . good luck. At least we don't have to go in on the first landings."

We had already been informed of our duties. Snipers rode in on the last waves with headquarters company after the grunts secured the beach.

"You'll go forward when the infantry gets pinned down and try to pick off the Jap positions," the captain told us. "That's what you're trained for, isn't it? We expect you to do your job. You'll get plenty of action."

At first light on Easter morning, the planes and naval guns of the huge armada gathered offshore began bombarding Okinawa. Laden with rifles and ammunition and filled packs, Marines crowded onto the decks of the transports and, while we waited for the word to go over the sides, watched the diving planes, the yellow flashes of the cruisers' guns, the long red streaks of shells arcing into the rising gray green hills above the beaches, the busy flash-blossoming of shells exploding. Clouds of black smoke billowed above the island like the worst kind of storm. I didn't see how any living thing could survive it.

"That's what we thought at Tarawa," somebody muttered glumly.

When the order came—"ready the landing force"— Carter and I flattened ourselves against the bulkhead out of the way, secretly relieved that we weren't among the first waves. Marines clambered down the rope nets like swarms of gray green ants. They stepped on the fingers and helmets of the men below them. Weapons clanged. Men sweated beneath the burden of machine guns and mortars. They ground their teeth and sweated and sometimes the tension made them curse or yell. They dropped the last few feet off the nets and caught the landing craft rising or falling with the swells. They crouched belly to back beneath the gunwales as the boats churned out to the assembly areas and circled and formed huge rings before finally fanning out into broad lines for the charge toward the beach. Their hulls dug deep into the water and kicked up frothing wakes that made the boats in succeeding waves buck and pitch. As far as you could see, waves of landing craft went plowing toward the beaches.

The sea was calm and the morning cool and just a little misty. You could see the control boats flying their colored flags off the beaches. They were the traffic cops. The naval guns kept pounding the hills above the beaches until the first amtracs almost reached the sand. Then they lifted. The thunder stopped, but the strike aircraft from the carriers kept diving like fierce bees into the billowing smoke. Their bombs crumped like strings of muffled firecrackers.

Landing craft disgorged troops and tanks onto the sand. We waited for the Japanese to open up. I watched through binoculars as the first Marine waves rushed to the sea wall of grass and threw themselves behind cover. After awhile, though, when nothing happened, they started standing up.

"Where the hell are the nips? The Japs—there aren't any Japs there!"

Someone said you could have mixed martinis and sipped them sitting on the sand. I'd have settled for a cold beer.

Within an hour after the landing started, what remained of the morning mist lifted and the sun burned down upon an incredible scene. Transports offshore continued to discharge more men and vehicles. Amphibs piled ashore and waddled up to the sea wall. Troops poured onto the sand. Marines and tanks and jeeps began moving up the slopes and through the grass toward the interior. Tropical breezes caught the black smoke left from the bombardment and whisked it away to expose the hills and bluffs. Spotter planes circling above to radio back progress reported no signs of the enemy.

Corporal Carter and I went ashore with headquarters. Everything seemed confused, as though the absence of a hot landing had thrown off everything, but soon we were troding up a narrow dirt road in trail of the infantry companies of the Fifth Marine Regiment, First Marines. The Sixth Marines also got themselves unscrambled and started toward the highlands, while south of the Bishi River the Seventh and Ninety-sixth Army Infantry Divisions were also beginning their push.

The First Marines went for a walk in the sun. We met few of the sixty thousand or so Japs the "Know Your Enemy" lectures aboard ship assured us were waiting and ready to defend the island to their deaths. All we encountered were small groups of Okinawan civilians, mostly old men, women, and children, which armed guards hustled to the rear. A platoon exchanged a few shots with a Japanese rear guard near the Yontan airfield, but otherwise we just walked into Yontan and the other airfield at Kadena and set up business. We marched all the way across the island to the Katchin Peninsula. I cased up my Springfield and soon felt so secure that at night I rolled into my poncho and slept soundly, in spite of the warnings that kept passing back and forth between the old hands.

"It's a trap. They're drawing us onto some kind of killing ground."

But it was the Army divisions in the south, and not

the Marines, that were drawn onto a killing ground. While the First Marines dug in on the Katchin Peninsula and waited in reserve and the Sixth Marines swept north, the Army encountered stiff resistance around Naha that soon turned into a *real* battle. Some nights, heavy artillery roared until daybreak.

For about thirty days I lay around on a hilltop occupied by headquarters and watched the American armada offshore bombard southern Okinawa. Occasionally, Kamikazes and Baka bombs attacked the ships. The Zero Kamikazes came in low and fast and tried to hurl themselves into a ship before they were shot out of the air; Japanese Betty bombers released the Bakas high in the air. The Bakas were nothing but bombs with wings on them and a suicide pilot. The pilot attempted to glide his one-way craft through the AA fire and crash it into a ship.

The battle was a long way off. You couldn't see the people, only the ships and airplanes and all the ack-ack and smoke in the air. It looked like a battle fought by toys. We watched from the hilltop and cheered and slapped each other on the back, like spectators at a football game, every time our side scored a point by blasting a Jap plane out of the air.

Then one day came the word that we had been dreading, inevitable as it was. *We* were going into that hell. The First Marines were moving south to relieve an Army infantry division that had got the hell kicked out of it along the Shuri Line, where the Japs in the mountains were fighting from cave to cave.

"This time," Carter said, "*really,* no more cow shit and yellow chalk."

I thought he was right, but getting ready this time didn't seem so bad as it had on the transports before the landing. I hadn't seen any actual personal combat,

72

but combat was all around me. It was like it wasn't so bad if you got used to it a little at a time.

Some of us rode six-bys, but most of us walked. We were strung off the hills and down from the Katchin Peninsula for miles, threading through the jungles and along barely discernible paths and roads like a trail of ants. On the second or third morning we entered terrain over which the battle had already swept. It resembled wreckage left behind by squads of drunken bulldozer drivers. Jap corpses lay scattered about like bunches of bloated dead cows. Disgusting clouds of black flies rose from the bodies as we passed. One or two guys puked when they found that the rice the nips spilled when they died *moved*.

The dogfaces started pulling back when we moved in. They were bloody and limping and ragged with that haunted look of war in their eyes that all men acquire during combat. It made me feel uneasy.

Artillery coughed day and night. It seemed the Japs always counterattacked around midnight. The fighting raged out ahead of headquarters. Snipers got the word to go forward whenever pockets of Jap snipers or machine gun nests pinned down our guys. You took a deep breath because you were going out there. Then you darted and crawled and fought your way from downed trees to splintered stumps to shell craters, through mud that was like a freshly plowed field after a downpour, working your way to the high ground if you could so you could shoot down into the enemy positions.

"Sniper up!"

The word kept coming back once our boys reached the Wana Gorge Valley. It was full of Jap nests. Nambu machine guns had a Marine company pinned down in the drizzle, chewing up the terrain around them and sometimes a gyrene, bottling up the entrance to the valley and clotting out the rest of the battalion.

"Sniper up!"

Carter cast me a glance as he slung his 20X spotting scope on a strap across his back and gave his Thompson .45 a quick check to make sure it wasn't plugged with mud. I stuck a .38 revolver in my pocket and led the way forward with my '03. Panting from exertion, we found our way to the top of a ridge overlooking the valley, all the time listening to the intermittent chatter of the Nambu as it grew louder the closer we got. Mud collected on our feet like twenty-pound weights. Fog clinging heavily to the peaks slithered into the lowlands and writhed in thin veils along stream beds and among the battered remains of forests.

Artillery shells had knocked down trees on top of the ridge. Some of them still smoldered. With Carter at my elbow, I crawled up and looked through a space. The Nambu let loose a string. I ducked instinctively, then looked again. I noticed sweat ran in rivulets from Carter's lean face. I felt myself sweating too.

"Sonofa . . ." Carter started.

I finished it for him: ". . . bitch!"

It was like having the front row seat to a movie. The voices of the Marines on the floor of the valley sounded thin and reedy as they were whipped into shreds by the rapid *Clack! Clack! Clack!* of the Japs' machine guns. Marines scurried among a field of shell craters and shattered forest; they sprawled motionless behind whatever cover they could find. A few of them lay in the open. They were dead. Nips high on the ridge opposite from us sprayed them with a deadly hail of lead.

"They're wiping us out!" Carter cried impulsively.

At least 1,200 yards of valley separated us from the machine gun nests. Fog made for such poor visibility that I could not tell where the firing came from. Desperately, I used my rifle scope to search for gun smoke or some movements to give the Japs away. Carter used his spotting scope. I saw caves and coral ledges and ragged stumps. Down in the valley a Marine jumped up to improve his position. An invisible finger fell out of the air and seemed to flip off his head. The body went tumbling and flopping.

That lent further desperation to our mission.

Carter spoke first: "I found them."

"Where?"

"There."

"Goddamnit, *where* there? There's a lot of *there* out there."

"See that cave, five o'clock from that telephone pole?"

I followed his point to a spot located just below a coral ledge honeycombed with shallow caves. The nest was well camouflaged and dug in, but I detected a thin screen of smoke coming from what appeared to be toppled underbrush. The smoke was a little bluer than that made by shellfire, and it was darker than the shredded remnants of fog. There was no wind; the gun smoke clung to the air above the boulders and felled trees. Pinpoint muzzle flame flickered from the shadows. Two, maybe three, guns were rattling from that location.

"I estimate twelve or thirteen hundred yards," Carter said, discouraged.

His voice trailed off into tension and a question mark. A lot of variables entered into shooting at a range of even one thousand yards, the longest shot I had ever tried. Wind and heat waves and, in this case, fog distorted the scope picture. The ammo we used was not match grade; it came right out of the green boxes. Sometimes you got misfires with it; sometimes a round simply went *poof!* and you had no idea which way it went.

I looked about frantically. The ridge we were on cut away from the valley the farther you went down it, increasing the range across. I saw I had no choice. The Japs were chewing up the Marines below us.

"We don't have time for anything else," I muttered and felt sweat popping from every pore in my body. "Whatever we do, it has to be done from *here*."

After some quick calculations, spurred on by hopelessness, I slipped a tracer round into the chamber of the Springfield and indicated to Carter that I was going to use the telephone pole above the enemy placements as an aiming stake to try to get the range. Carter glued his eye to his spotting scope.

"Pick her up an inch!" he curtly advised after my first shot.

The pinned-down Marines couldn't spare the time. I adjusted the scope elevation knob and dropped cross hairs onto the Japanese machine gun nest. The nips had to expose themselves at least a little in order to pivot their gun barrels down toward the valley floor. I heard Carter murmur something about cow shit and yellow chalk as I narrowed my concentration against a tiny patch of grayish uniform exposed above a tree trunk. I tried to remember everything I had learned at Camp Pendleton about long-distance shooting. So much depended on it.

Smoke curled up from behind the logs as the Nambu commenced to chatter its short repetitive phrases.

Deep breath. Let half out. Hold. Cross-hair, crosshair, squeeze.

With the spotter scope, you could actually pick up the streak of the bullet going through the air. Carter grunted. "All *right*," he said when my first round plunged into the enemy's barricade.

"Give it to the little yellow bastards!"

I worked the bolt with a feeling of elation. My hands and breathing were surprisingly steady. I fired and worked the bolt, fired and worked the bolt, pouring accurate fire into the Japanese defenses, cross-hairing handkerchief-sized targets momentarily exposed more than a half mile away. Even through his spotting scope, Carter couldn't tell when I scored because the targets were so fleeting they disappeared whether I made a hit or not, but he was all grins.

The machine gun fire ceased.

Then: "They're running!"

Several minute figures scurried from the barricades like rats smoked out of a barn. I released a parting shot as they vanished over the ridge top. That was when I took a deep, wavering breath. I remembered what the captain said before we left the ship: "We expect you to do your job."

I had done my job, hadn't I?

Below on the valley floor, Marines were starting to clamber cautiously to their feet. They stood for a minute, half crouched, rifles and eyes pointing in the direction of the silenced enemy, as though not quite believing it. Presently, they regrouped and began slogging forward again, spread out across the valley. One of them turned and waved thanks back at us.

Their CO later told me I had stacked up some Jap corpses. I felt good about it. I had done some damned good shooting. Carter said there'd be other occasions for some more damned good shooting before this war ended.

He was right too. We were still fighting on Okinawa on May 8, 1945, when Germany fell. The island seemed to take a deep sigh, as though unsure of where this left it. At exactly noon, every gun on the island and every ship's gun fired one shot to celebrate V-E

Day. I fired my victory round across a marsh at a battered tree trunk. It was a good one thousand yards away. I hit it, too.

Then we got up and pushed on. It was terrible weather. Rain turned the island into bloody mush. I had trouble keeping mud from gumming up my rifle scope.

"No more yellow chalk and cow shit," Carter said.

I didn't even look up.

CHAPTER SEVEN

Just before daybreak one morning during the summer of 1952, the commander of Third Battalion, First Marines, waited in an outpost bunker for enough light so that he could glass the terrain in front of his stalemated battalion. After the Americans had first been pushed back nearly into the sea and then regained lost ground due to MacArthur's daring landing at Inchon, the Korean front had assumed all the characteristics of World War I trench warfare—static, muddy, a war of attacks and counterattacks and attrition that gained little other than inflated body counts. Captain Herbert McBride in France nearly a half century before would have understood this war.

As first light eased cautiously above the distant mountains to wash a pale sheen over the faces of the battlefield's shell-scarred slopes, the CO raised his binoculars to gaze out the bunker opening. *Ping!* Almost instantly, a sniper's bullet smashed the glasses and sent the officer reeling back with a wounded hand.

Although the wound was only a scratch, it was to have a great deal of significance for Third Battalion.

The commander was fuming as he nursed his wound. "It's a helluva situation when the CO can't even take a look at the terrain he's defending without getting shot at!" he raved. "Something has got to be done about those goddamned snipers."

What he decided was that the Third Battalion needed snipers who could outsnipe the enemy snipers, marksmen with infinite patience who could wait indefinitely for an enemy head to appear and who, when it did appear, could hit it every time at five hundred yards.

In static warfare, it is in the sniper's power to dominate his own sector's front. One hard-shooting sniper is worth more than a pair of light machine gun crews. His killing power is extensive and ubiquitous, plus the psychological factor of the single accurate shot cracking from nowhere lowers the enemy's morale and makes him afraid to take chances. Snipers further provided the added benefit of intelligence gathering. Almost nothing the enemy does goes unnoticed when four good snipers waiting for a target lie on a battalion's front observing the enemy through scopes.

The numerous sniper schools that had mushroomed to fill the need for specialized marksmen during World War II had all been discontinued after the Axis surrendered. Snipers had been needed, they were used, and now it was better not to talk about such cold killers in the rational light of peace. Nonetheless, as soon as there was war again, the CO of Third Battalion wasn't the only officer to conclude that Korea needed snipers. As the Americans and South Koreans dug in for the long ordeal along the Thirty-eighth Parallel, commanding officers of every line unit of company size or larger began forming sniper units. Although there were few official guidelines, the commanders relied upon lessons passed down from the World Wars in selecting, organizing, and training their marksmen.

As before, they wanted good infantry riflemen who, above all else, possessed the essential patience to remain still and alert for long periods of time waiting for a target. The Third Battalion was typical of most in the way it trained and deployed its snipers. It selected six two-man teams per company and sent them a few hundred yards behind the MLR (Main Line of Resistance) for three weeks' training. The men built their own firing ranges out of whatever was available and held training lectures in spite of what might be happening at the front lines only a short distance away.

Students trained with either the .30-caliber M-1, modified into a sniper's weapon called the M-1D, or with the 1903 Springfield, according to preference. Lieutenant Colonel Glen Martin, who helped set up a sniper program for the Fifth Marines, recommended the '03 mainly because of its more powerful 8X Unertl scope, bolt action, and increased accuracy at longer ranges. While both rifles were adequate at 700 yards, sometimes stretching to 1,000 yards, neither proved entirely satisfactory for the ultra long-range Korean terrain. What the snipers wanted was a weapon they could use on one mountain top to pick off Chinese and North Korean soldiers on another mountain top, something like the single-shot .50-caliber produced on the foreign market and used by other governments as an antitank weapon.

What they settled for was a scope mounted on the .50 Browning machine gun, which could be fired single shot and which was effective at ranges up to and beyond twelve hundred yards. In Korea, however, the ground-mounted machine gun proved too bulky and cumbersome and was never widely used in sniping.

According to the Marine Corps, it was not until Vietnam that the .50 caliber machine gun with a 10X scope was established as a sniper weapon. Although it was not widely used even there, the longest single-shot kill ever made by a sniper was made using the Browning .50.

Sergeant Carlos Hathcock made it while operating off a hillside overlooking a wide flat valley near Duc Pho during Operation Desota. He shot a VC "mule"—an arms runner—off a bicycle with one shot at twenty-five hundred meters—more than one and one-half miles away!

Some American snipers in the Korean War, as in previous wars, received no formal sniper training at all. They were selected based merely on their shooting scores from boot camp, issued scoped rifles, and told to go forward and pick off the enemy. Others finished courses ranging from two days to three weeks and returned to their respective companies where they occupied camouflaged outpost bunkers. The First Marines offered a cold case of beer to the snipers of each outpost who managed to rack up twelve kills within any one week. It wasn't long before the hard-shooting Marine marksmen remedied a situation in which enemy snipers seemed to be in control of the MLR.

"In nothing flat there was no more sniping on our positions," the Third Battalion CO recalled. "Nothing moved out there but what we hit it."

The division commander inspected the lines. Where barely a week before men dared not stick up their heads, even for an instant, the two-star general sauntered the length of Item Company's MLR, armed with nothing but a walking stick.

"By God, it works!" he exclaimed. "What we need on this front are more snipers."

Different units employed their snipers in different ways, limited only by the imagination. During an attack, snipers were used to fire through gaps between assaulting squads and to force the enemy to remain under cover. They were sent to outposts on the defense to plink at targets of opportunity. When their own lines were attacked, they pulled back to open accurate fire and make the enemy get into attack formation early. They operated on intelligence-gathering patrols and sometimes went out to harass the enemy.

The Fifth Marines organized their snipers into squads, with four two-man teams, or eight snipers, to each squad. On May 21, 1952, Lieutenant Gil Holmes' battalion moved into position to stem an enemy penetration attempt. Enemy soldiers moved across the battalion front at a distance of one thousand yards. The Marine battalion on the left flank had been heavily assaulted earlier. Holmes was ordered to take a reconnaisance patrol consisting of two rifle squads and four sniper teams into no-man's-land to determine the limit of the enemy's forward movement and to harass the Reds as much as possible.

A rifle squad traveled on each flank to cover the sniper teams as the patrol slipped into the pulverized terrain lighted by a weak spring sun. Taking advantage of cover, the patrol stole down washouts and streams and crawled around the friendly side of hills. The Marines crept cautiously to within four hundred yards of the entrenched enemy on Hill 719.

"The scout-sniper patrol left its two reinforcing squads at a vantage point on high ground about three hundred yards outside Dog Company's lines," Lieutenant Holmes reported, "because we felt such a large force would preclude our hopes for a surprise attack. Throughout the course of our approach to Hill 719, our objective was always in plain sight and a certain amount of enemy activity could be observed on the skyline as we made our way forward.

"Naturally we took full advantage of the defilade and concealment available, but I will never cease to wonder how we got so close to the main battle positions without detection. After we were ordered to break contact and withdraw I do recall that we were momentarily caught in an automatic cross-fire from both flanks and, if I am any judge of such matters, it did not come from the Chinese MLR so it is barely possible that we did penetrate a very thin screening force without knowing it.

"We finally reached a ridge top roughly parallel to the entrenchments on 719 from which we could look across and see a couple of Chinese wandering around the area in an unconcerned manner. I would say that the range from our position was about four hundred yards. As we made our approach an L-5 hovered overhead, and finally made a few passes at 719.

"This action obviously irritated the enemy and they opened fire from the reverse slope with a machine gun. After several low passes, the plane shoved off, and I decided to get down to business.

"We were all spread along the ridge in a loose skirmish line with sights adjusted, waiting for renumerative targets. I finally spotted three at the same time and gave the word to cut loose. That really did it!

"I had no idea what a hornet's nest they had over there. They came running out of their bunkers along the trench to their battle stations, but it soon was obvious they were rather fouled up.

"They tried to set up a machine gun to our direct front and one of my boys knocked off the gunner. When they finally got the gun in action they opened up on an area at least two hundred yards from our left flank. Some joker, evidently the company commander, was running around like a madman trying to square things away, but his people were crumbling up all around him under a steady stream of the well-aimed fire of our sharpshooters.

"Soon after we opened fire, Dog Company called us back in. I stuck my neck out and held the position for another fifteen minutes after receiving the order because we had good shooting and the Chinese just couldn't seem to get squared away. They returned fire, but it was ineffective—they didn't seem to have a fix on our positions.

"At this point Dog Company warned us that the Chinese had commenced an envelopment in strength along a trail off our right flank which ran roughly perpendicular to our ridge. The enemy return fire was increasing in volume from 719, and inasmuch as there were only nine of us I decided it was time to obey orders. I'm sure we'd have done well if we'd engaged the enveloping force, but with no corpsmen available we'd have had a rough time getting out if someone had been hit.

"As we pulled out we received automatic weapon cross-fire from our flanks, but it was well overhead. I figured there was a fair chance we'd be intercepted on the way in, so we withdrew by bounds—half covering the other half.

"Approximately three-quarters of an hour after we broke contact and commenced our withdrawal from 719 we were safely back inside our own lines without spilling a drop of Marine blood—it was a good day!"

CHAPTER EIGHT

U.S. Army Corporal
Chet Hamilton
Korea, 1952

We were going to the front lines. At the Seventh Division replacement depot in Inchon, they loaded up the new guys on trains and then trucks and we sped out across rice fields and places where, from all the damage it was obvious the war had already been, toward the mountains where the lines had bogged down on both sides. There had been talks of truce meetings, but no one expected any quick results. While the talks went on, the way I understood it, the Americans and the chinks were going at it at places like Old Baldy and Pork Chop Hill in a deadly kind of shadowboxing. They hit us, we hit them, they hit us back. It just kept going like that.

I was a tall, lean, redheaded kid, twenty years old, when I joined Baker Company in the vicinity of Pike's Peak. It wasn't until Baker moved to the western part of the area around Pork Chop Hill that somebody learned I had been firing on the Sixteenth Rangers rifle team back in the U.S. and that I could shoot. Since I was the only man in the company with any rifle team or shooting experience, the CO called back and requested a sniper rifle for me.

"Hamilton, that makes you the company sniper," he said.

The sniper rifle was a brand-new M-1C with a 4X scope and a cheek pad. It was packed in cosmoline. I had a helluva time scrubbing off all that cosmoline with the little can of kerosene that came with the weapon. I zeroed it in on a discarded grenade flare case, then peered across at the Chinese trenches that were only about 140 yards away at the nearest point. I was a sniper.

Baker Company was sent out to the twin outpost hills of Erie and Arsenal, thrust far out into the Yokkokchon Valley from the main line across the higher ridges. Isolated positions like these, engineered for defense and encircled by broad fields of wire, formed an outwork all along the Eighth Army front. They were always within artillery and 4.2 mortar range. Trucks kept them supplied over dirt roads during the daylight, but at night everything buttoned down.

Arsenal was the forward hill at the extreme end of the ridge, while Erie in the rear about 440 yards guarded over it. The crowns of both hills were stoutly fortified with bunkers heavily timbered and thickly sandbagged. They were virtually artillery resistant. You could get into a trench at Erie and cross over to Arsenal.

Tactically, the outposts looked weak. That was intentional. The object was to tempt the communists with a soft touch in an effort to lure them into the open where they could be pounded to pieces by U.S. artillery. Because any infantry on the hills were hardly more than pawns, it was extraordinarily hazardous duty.

One of the Baker platoons settled in at Erie, while the other two platoons took Arsenal. I was getting in almost no shooting, certainly not what I had been led to expect. That was because the Chinese had been fortifying their positions for almost two years. Their trenches were a maze that presented few targets. There were no easily identifiable gun positions, dumps, OPs, LPs, communications centers. Their system of fighting trenches led into subterranean tunnels big enough to house battalions against attacks. The trenches seemed to be manned only by lookouts whose duty it was to alert the garrison of any attack. Rarely did you see anyone.

As soon as the sun went down, two gigantic Air Force-type searchlights on a hill about a mile behind us came on and bathed the valley in bright light and sharp, dark shadows. The lights shined directly on the outposts, but all the chinks could see looking toward us were those miniature suns burning in their eyes. We shined lights on them. They played martial music back at us over loudspeakers. It was a hellish combination.

One night I was looking through my rifle scope across the valley to the chink positions on the opposite hill when something flashed in the wash of the Air Force searchlights. I kept looking until I saw the head of a shovel. One of the Reds was doing a little home improvement, digging in his trench and throwing the dirt up on top of the berm. He patted down each shovelful twice with the shovel before going back for more.

I couldn't resist it. The next time the shovel came up and started to pat, I put a bullet through it. I heard the bullet strike the metal. The shovel vibrated and hummed in the Chicom's hands. It must have shook his teeth loose. He didn't do any more digging that night.

Two weeks later, while Baker was still on the outposts, word came that GIs from our line were going to counterattack the Chinese who occupied positions around the two horseshoe-shaped hills to our front where I had shot the shovel. The attack was going to use three rifle platoons supported by tanks.

From our hills, we heard the company assembling in attack formation behind us, under cover, and we heard the tanks' motors, although we couldn't see anything. At first light, our artillery rained artillery shells with VT (Variable Timed Fuses) on the hills, four minutes on and four off, and a cloud of dust shook loose by the shells towered sixty feet in the air. The infantry came sweeping around out of cover and went double timing across the open valley between Arsenal and Erie and the Chinese hill. It looked like two platoons on line with a third in reserve and a half-dozen tanks lumbering along in front. The tank guns opened up on the hills as the American VT lifted.

All the grass and trees and shrubbery on the battlefield had been shelled into matchsticks and toothpicks. All that remained out there was a dirty moonscape of shell craters and debris from all the fighting littered across a rocky surface. The Chinese held the high ground. They poured withering fire right down into the GIs' faces; GIs started dropping everywhere. You could hear the wounded screaming above the din of the battle.

The GIs who made it to the hill started up the slope. The grade was so steep they tugged at rocks and bushes to assist them. The more heavily burdened with machine guns and flame throwers straggled, while skirmishers broke into little pockets to continue the assault.

I felt helpless watching from the sandbagged trenches on Erie until I noticed something. It was only about four hundred yards across the valley from the Chinese lines. My position put me on almost the same level with the chink defenders on the other hill. In order for the Chicoms to see our troops and fire at them down through their wire as the GIs charged up the hill, they had to lean up and out over their trenches, exposing wide patches of their quilted hides.

That was all I needed.

It had become a clear morning in spite of the smoke and dust boiling above the Chinese hill. The four-power magnification of my scope made the chinks leap right into my face. All I had to do was go down the trench line, settle the post-and-horizontal-line reticle on one target right after the other, and squeeze the trigger. It was a lot like going to a carnival and shooting those little toy crows off the fence. *Bap!* The crow disappeared and you moved over to the next crow. By the time you got to the end of the fence, you came back to the beginning and the crows were all lined up again ready for you to start over. I don't know who the Chinese first sergeant was over there, but he kept throwing up another crow for me every minute or two. And I kept knocking them off the fence. The fight for the hill lasted about two hours. I was busy for the full time. The other guys on Erie came to watch, point out targets, and cheer when I zapped one.

The GIs never made it past the chink wire. Heavy Chinese mortar and artillery fire stopped the advance and started cutting the infantry to pieces. The tanks scurried for cover when the artillery fire singled them out; they weren't much benefit on the steep grade anyhow. By the time the GIs withdrew from the hill, dashing from rock to rock, demoralized and defeated, my gun barrel was so hot to the touch that I could hardly touch it. You could smell the cosmoline being cooked out of the metal. I know I shot at least forty chinks before the attack bogged down and the enemy went back to their burrows. Bodies had to be stacked up in the Chinese trenches.

I wondered if the first sergeant over there ever figured out what happened.

CHAPTER NINE

U.S. Marine Corporal
Ernest R. Fish
Korea, 1951

During the summer and fall of 1951, the lines in Korea became static with the First Marine Division opposite the North Korean Army. We hadn't yet moved over to the other side of the peninsula against the Red Chinese Army. Winter was coming on. You could taste it in the morning when the wind blew right out of the north. When there was no wind, hoar frost dusted your parka and helmet and pinched your nose and made your trigger finger stiff.

Someone up the chain of command decided that what each line company needed was a sniper. The gunnies checked our SRBs (Service Record Books) to see who had the highest range scores. I qualified with a 237 out of a possible 250 on the Chappo Flat Range at Camp Pendleton.

"Fish, pull your ass out of that hole," the company gunny said. "You're going to sniper school, lad."

I learned some of the battalions had really good

schools, especially later on, but this one we treated as a joke. Anyhow, it got us out of the trenches for awhile, and that was good enough for me. A few of us with a gunny as an instructor got up one morning and had C-rats for breakfast and hiked back to a valley in the rear with a high brown hill at the end of it between us and the front lines. We stood around and slapped our sides to keep warm and blew clouds of breath until somebody trucked out some fifty-gallon metal fuel drums painted white. We looked them over and grinned.

One of the students said, "Them slant-eyes ain't nowhere near as big as them barrels—unless they got a lot fatter since the last one I seen. And ain't none of 'em painted white so you can see 'em."

The six-by truck chugged out across the rocky flats against the hill and we placed the white barrels at staggered intervals. There was one at 100 yards and so on up to 500 yards. The gunny issued us standard M-1s to which armorers had attached 2½X Weaver scopes. We felt a little slighted when we heard Army snipers were using bolt-action 1903 Springfields with 10X scopes, but we were told we couldn't get any of those. Big as those barrels were, it was still just plain Missouri luck if you hit them at 500 yards using that 2½X scope.

We all laid down on the ground and fired at the barrels while the gunny stood and looked through field glasses. After the clips *pinged!* empty, we grinned confidently at each other and got up and sauntered out to count the holes in the barrels. The grins turned sheepish as we approached the more distant barrels and found maybe only one or two holes in them.

It was hard to tell who put which holes where, although the gunny tried to keep score using his field glasses. We tried tracers for awhile, but they burned out after a couple of hundred yards.

"Dammit, Fish. That's *my* hole," someone joked. "*You* couldn't hit a bull in the ass with a bass fiddle."

We bivouacked in the valley shooting at the barrels for a week and getting used to the scopes. By the end of the week, we were putting quite a few more holes in the distant barrels than we were at the beginning. It started snowing and got so cold the lenses on the scopes fogged up every few seconds. The gunny declared us ready to go back on the line and shoot slant-eyes. I felt ready.

Before we left, we were issued white trousers and a white parka with a white hood and gloves. The gunny showed us how to spiral white tape around our rifles to break up the outline.

"What can be *seen* can be hit," he said. "That goes for them same as for you."

I was gung ho and ready to do some shooting. The way we were supposed to operate was that a fire team would escort a sniper as close as possible to enemy lines without going out far enough to get cut off. Most of the time, the closest we could get was maybe thirteen hundred yards, sometimes closer, but seldom within good effective range of the M-1. What with the fire team escort, there were too many of us crawling around out there in the snow together to try to get any closer. We looked like a bunch of clumsy polar bears, more suited for being targets than finding targets.

Before daybreak each morning, we sneaked out to get set up. I lay in the snow and used field glasses to study the North Korean defensive line. It consisted of well-camouflaged bunkers connected by a continuous trench across the front of a barren snow-swept mountain. We snipers were supposed to harass the enemy, but there were too many things against us. We couldn't crawl close enough without the fire team escort being spotted, it was so cold that you stuck to the ground if you lay there too long, and the North Koreans seldom showed themselves during the day.

I lay in the snow two or three hours every day trying to get a shot, staying out as long as I could without getting hypothermia. The fire team tried to find shelter behind rocks and hills and still cover me. Every day the other snipers and I came slinking home in defeat. I went to the gunny about it.

"Let me try it out there by myself. I think I can get close enough then."

"Corporal Fish, I am not having one of my men going nowhere by himself and getting himself killed so I have to write home to his widow."

"Gunny, I been out there every day for two weeks and I ain't even *seen* a slant-eye. How can I shoot 'em if I can't see 'em?"

"Corporal, if you see 'em, you shoot 'em. If you don't, you don't. One man ain't gonna win this war by himself even if he does have a scope on his Garand."

" I got the same bullet in my rifle I started with."

Discouraged, I started cutting down on the amount of time I spent on the snow in no-man's-land. My escorts didn't like being out there anyhow.

"I still got the same bullet," I told the gunny.

When I finally got the chance for some action, it was such a surprise to me that precious seconds elapsed before I reacted. I was scanning the enemy trenches like always when an enemy soldier in an off-white quilted coat suddenly stood up on the side of his trench and gazed in my direction. Maybe he thought he saw something and wanted to make sure.

My heart started pounding. I could hear it in my temples. I was in such a rush to get rid of my first bullet, now that I had the opportunity, that I was afraid I was getting buck fever.

I took a deep breath to steady my nerves.

Everything was against me. The scope lenses were cloudy with cold. I slipped my shooting finger free of its mitten and it stiffened almost immediately. It was hard to determine range across snow, but I estimated the distance at eight hundred yards. That was a long shot even on a warm, windless day.

As I sighted my cross hairs on the Korean, lifting them at that distance to his head to compensate for bullet drop and zeroing at 500 yards, a disconcerting thought unexpectedly entered my head. I saw the white barrels in the valley and I remembered how few holes ever appeared in the ones at 500 yards.

This slant-eye staring right into my scope, making balloons with his breath, was nowhere near as big as a barrel.

The crack of the rifle sounded flat and startling across the snow field. When I looked again after the recoil, the Korean was gone.

Of course, he was gone.

"You got rid of your bullet today, huh, Fish?" the gunny cracked when I got back to the lines. "You got one?"

All I could think about were the far barrels.

CHAPTER TEN

U.S. Army Sergeant
Chet Hamilton
Korea, 1953

Around Korea's Pork Chop Hill and Old Baldy it was so cold on January 19, the day I turned twenty-one, that when you took a leak it turned to ice before it hit the ground. The shadowboxing was still going on, and so were the truce talks. The chinks hit us and we hit them back and the war went on like that back and forth with neither side gaining or losing much.

I looked around for a dead Chinaman. Most of them wore padded quilted green uniforms. They were quite warm. Some of the Mongolians were six feet tall with crew-cut hair and wore white towels around their heads and bags of rice around their necks. They carried opium pipes in their pockets, PpSH-41 burp guns with drum magazines and wooden stocks. It seemed like they could fire about a thousand rounds per minute. They had two types of grenades—the small pineapple type with the stick handle and the large antitank grenade with a sheet metal body. They could blow a bunker completely in.

When I found a dead Mongolian about my size, I pulled off his pants since he wouldn't need them anymore, and wore them underneath my own.

The main line of friendly resistance looped across three ridges to the south of Old Baldy and Pork Chop. The center of these ridges stuck out like a finger into a valley. Off the end of the finger was a hill and an outpost on top of the hill called Dale, named after a lieutenant who got killed. A commo trench connected it back to the MLR on the finger. The top of the hill was no larger than half the size of a football field. No other friendly ground was closer to the enemy than Dale. It was only about three hundred yards across a valley to the Chinese trenches.

When Baker Company moved down on the line and my platoon occupied Dale, I scoped the chink trenches all the time on Hill 222 and 190-Able that were out in front of us, trying to pick out a target. Between us and the hills, the valley was full of shellfire pits and blasted tree stumps that looked like men marching in the moonlight and caused GIs to waste a lot of ammo and artillery fire. I even picked off one or two stumps myself, but the only time the Chinese showed themselves was when they were actually making an attack. What we heard was that a company of chinks occupied Hill 222 by living in a great chamber cut into the mountain from the rear.

I hadn't got in much sniper shooting since the GI counterattack past Erie outpost.

In some of the other sectors, the Chinese blew bugles to signal an attack, but in my sector they yelled and used flares. In the beginning, the Chinese picked up old men and kids as they moved south and used them as buffers. The unarmed civilians were driven out ahead in an attack, followed by the first wave of soldiers throwing grenades. The next wave had burp guns. Sometimes the next two waves didn't have any weapons at all. Instead, they had pocketfuls of American ammunition. During a fight you could see them wandering around trying to find dead Americans so they could pick up their weapons and use them against us.

We did everything we could to keep the Chinese off us. Our positions were underground with overhead cover made of logs and sandbags six to eight feet thick. They would take blasts from everything except the real heavy stuff. When the Chinese, attacking with thirty times the number of troops we had, overran Dale, we buttoned up and called in artillery with VT fuses directly on top of us to blast the chinks off. The artillery was already preplotted; you just radioed in and said "Queen" or "Jack" or "Dale" and told what you wanted and the gunners gave it to you. We called in artillery on ourselves more than once.

When you looked out one of the bunker firing slits, what you saw were three or four layers of concertina wire unraveled down the slopes. C-rat cans filled with pebbles—early warning devices—dangled from the wire like Christmas tree ornaments.

One night I was in the wire laying out booby traps of WP (White Phosphorous) and frag grenades. The searchlights were blazing away in the Chinamen's eyes, but I kept glancing over my shoulder at the enemy trenches while I worked. Apparently, the chinks could see me, because a shot cracked from across the valley and the bullet kicked up a geyser of dirt about five feet from me. I saw the Chinaman who did it. I whirled toward him and couldn't think of anything else but to shake my fist at him. He dropped and I didn't see him again.

There were three hills in the Old Baldy area—what we called East View, West View, and Old Baldy itself. Trenches connected them. You almost needed a road map. A trench ran from East View to West View and on up to the crest of Old Baldy. Months of battle had turned the area into a refuse dump. Old Baldy was too naked and steep to offer any kind of concealment, so the only cover getting to the top were the trenches.

In March, a battalion of Colombian UN troops and five of our Sherman tanks were holding Old Baldy when the Chicoms hit the hill with about 3,000 troops and wiped out all except 25 men and one tank crew. The surviving infantry escaped back to friendly lines, but the tank crew survived by bottling up inside the disabled tank.

Baker Company was standing in reserve at the time. The searchlights went out and a moonless night closed over East View. The company commander passed down the word that two platoons would be sent up to Old Baldy to check things out and maybe regain it. By then I was a platoon sergeant as well as the company sniper; the platoon took precedence. I traded my scoped M-1 for a .30-caliber carbine and got the platoon ready to go.

"Plenty of ammo," I said. "Take some C-rats. We might not get resupply for awhile."

No one needed to be told that anymore.

There had been a snow and it melted, leaving ankle-deep mud everywhere that froze over in a crust at night. My platoon took the lead, with Second Platoon trailing as we single-filed along the trenches from East View over to West View. There was no talking. We crested West View where we saw the darker end of Pork Chop Hill outlined against the stars farther east and beyond Old Baldy. There had been plenty of activity in the sector both before and since Old Baldy fell. We heard firing behind us, in the direction of Dale outpost. The CO halted the column so we could talk things over, whispering. The chinks had patrols out in force everywhere.

"If that's Dale, the Chinese may be cutting off our rear."

That was the big concern. Still, we had our orders. We continued along the trench toward Old Baldy. All you could see was the guy ahead of you, just his outline, and then the lighter demarcation where the lip of the trench met the sky. I was sure the Chinese could hear the tramp of about forty booted feet crunching the ice and the clanking of M-1s and light .30-caliber machine guns.

The trench climbed up the lower left slope of Old Baldy. About halfway up the hill, a private in the line stumbled and fell.

"Oh, good God!"

The terror in his voice carried up and down the column, but somebody grabbed him and hushed him immediately. The trench was full of dead Chinese. Stumbling over one of them, the private had stuck his hand wrist-deep into a pile of half-frozen intestines. The farther we proceeded in the trench, the thicker the corpses became. The Colombians had made a good accounting of themselves. Blood and shit and guts made the footing slippery, but soon the bodies were so thick it was easier to walk on them than to try to avoid them.

There was a T at the trench where it curved around and started back up to the crest of Old Baldy. Someone thought he saw something move across the opening at the joining of the T. By the time the word got back to the rear of the element, men were bunching up and wondering what was going on. I was rushing to the head of the column when a burp gun let out a burst and a swarm of bullets splattered against one wall of the trench. Half the men fell on their faces among the dead Chinese, while the other half ducked and looked around. Another Chinese at the T sprayed down our section of the trench with his burp gun. Several soldiers opened up in reply. Muzzle flashes flickered. Officers and NCOs started yelling.

"Hold your fire! Goddamnit! We'll shoot each other!"

We managed to get the men away from the T, leaving a forward light machine gun and a rifleman to cover it and keep the enemy from entering our part of the trenches. By then, firing had broken out in the trenches that we had just traversed between West View and Old Baldy. GIs moving in to reoccupy West View were apparently engaged with Chinese that had skirmished in between us and them. GIs looked at each other in the darkness of the short section of trench we held on the steeply sloping face of Old Baldy. Ahead of us, an unknown number of Chinese occupied the crossing of our T where they could poke their heads up over the earthworks and cut down on us. Behind us, our escape route had been cut.

Someone finally said it: "The cocksuckers got us trapped!"

I don't know who it was, but somebody else eased the tension. "Yep," went a Texas drawl, "now we got 'em right where we want 'em."

We managed to reach the CP on the radio. The CP told us to hold what we had until relieved. We mounted our defenses the best we could in the trench section we held and dug in until dawn might tell us more about the situation. The Chinese mostly fought at night.

Dawn lightened the sky, but failed to enlighten our situation much. As far as we could tell, the chinks still had us cut off from below, while an unknown number of them held our T-cross above. But those at the T-cross proved to be every bit as much in *our* trap as we were in *theirs*.

Peeking over the lip of the trench told us that artillery fire had caved in a long portion of their trench between them and the top of the hill. In order to escape, which the chinks obviously had in mind since two of them tried it just before the sun came up, they had to run uphill across a long open stretch to where the undamaged trench started again. The two that broke for it were pumping their arms like crazy, but couldn't work up any momentum. They were about a hundred yards away. I sighted in on the one in the lead. My bullet knocked him flat on the ground.

Seeing his comrade go down, the second one panicked. He didn't know what to do. He took a few more steps, then hesitated before he turned and started back down. By then I had my sights on him. He flopped around in the mud a few seconds before he died.

Later, more tried it. I picked off two more. Their bodies lay out there on the naked face and it misty-rained on them and snowed on them at night. There were so many bloated up and lying around, though, that you could barely tell the ones I killed from any of the others. Nobody else tried to make a run for it though. The Chinese settled down to hold their end of the trench, and we settled down to hold ours. We weren't more than fifty yards apart. (We fought each other at opposite ends of the same trench like that for a week.) We couldn't get away, but they couldn't get away either, because I or one of the others good with a rifle picked them off whenever they tried.

It turned into a stalemate. Chicoms in front of us fought a little every day and night, mostly just fast skirmishes of one or two shooting at one or two, until we started running out of ammo and had to use Chinese weapons we picked off the dead, while Chicoms behind us were fighting somebody else. Neither side had the strength or will to overwhelm the other, and apparently both lines were willing to leave us out here to solve our own problems. To charge out of the trench at each other was suicide; to attempt to fight our way past the T inside the trench was equally suicidal. So, we held and skirmished and burned up ammo.

The stench of the rotting dead grew overpowering. We fought from what was literally a mass grave. A few of us were wounded. The medics patched them up and they sat hunkered like zombies against the trench walls, waiting for something to resolve itself. The rest of us shivered at night and tried to catch a few winks of sleep in between keeping an eye open for enemy skullduggery.

None of us would have begrudged the trapped Chinese their escape except for one thing. As long as we kept them bottled down in the trench with us, their artillery kept silent. But even that was too good to last forever.

As the stalemate dragged on, the chink command grew tired of it and opened up on us with cannon and mortars. The first barrage sounded like new Chevrolets being hurled through the air. The earth rose and fell around us and a cloud of pulverized dust billowed into the air. We couldn't see each other in the trench. We hugged the ground and listened to the wounded and waited until each barrage ended before we regrouped and tended to the wounded.

The shelling continued. One part of the trench that had been seven feet deep was only four inches deep. It must have been just as devastating to the trapped chinks, maybe even more so. After all, it was their own guns that were burying them.

Our lines finally sent out a rescue attempt that

managed to open an escape route. Bloodied and demoralized, the platoons limped back to the MLR. Two weeks later, I ran a support patrol up the center of Old Baldy to the top where the Colombians had been wiped out. The trapped tank crewmen were still inside what they felt must surely be their coffin. A GI crawled underneath the tank and banged on the bottom with his helmet. Chinese didn't wear helmets. The trapped tankers had been playing 'possum for almost three weeks by this time. They stuck to us like glue until we got them off Old Baldy and back to our lines.

The Korean War was like this for most GI snipers. Being a sniper was a part-time job, something you did when you weren't out on patrols. While the peace-truce talks were continuing at Panmunjom, the deadly shadowboxing continued around Old Baldy and Pork Chop Hill. I made only a few more scoped shots at distant targets in the Chinese lines before the night of May 14, 1953, when Lieutenant Roland Ferris and I led the patrol that S.L.A. Marshall called "The Hexed Patrol" in his book *Pork Chop Hill*.

Ferris died when the Chinese overran us on Queen Knob, where we had set up as security for an ambush along a narrow river below. The Chinese hit us hard at about 9 P.M. with grenades and automatic weapons. The first bursts shattered my left elbow, killed the lieutenant and two other GIs, and wounded one or two others of the nine-man squad. We were on perimeter defense in a depression about two or three feet deep.

We poured fire on the chinks and drove the rush back. We were fighting in all directions. The fight lasted for over an hour before we started running out of ammo. It was either attempt to break out or die where we were. I grabbed Corporal Dee Thompson, who was shot up worse than me, and we left the dead and broke out at a run downhill to the right. Bullets were swarming. I bayoneted a Chicom who jumped in front of me, but then another chink shot me through the left hip with a burp gun. Running and stumbling, fighting as we retreated, I also caught some grenade shrapnel before we reached the ford at the stream and escaped to our lines.

I was still in Walter Reed Hospital in July when the war ended.

CHAPTER ELEVEN

Two men armed with bolt-action rifles slipped silently into a jungle hide deep inside Viet Cong territory. They settled down to wait. Any unnecessary movement might disclose their position. They spoke only in an occasional whisper. They did not smoke. Sometimes they waited as long as ten to twelve hours like that in order to release a single accurate shot at an elusive enemy. They had adopted a weapon borrowed from the VC, who had in turn borrowed it from the Japanese and others from as far back as men had gunpowder and realized the advantage of killing from hiding at a distance—the rifle that cracks from nowhere to bring sudden death.

Vietnam, with its lack of combat lines, its fluid battlefields, and an enemy that often operated singly or in small units, presented itself as the ideal setting for classic sniper warfare, even more so than the trenches of World War I or the more conventional set-piece actions of World War II. Korea had never been a true sniper's war.

After Korea, as at the end of each of its previous wars, the U.S. quickly ridded itself of any surviving sniper programs, again as though realizing that sniping and backshooting once the emergency was over was not a *High Noon* way of conducting war. As a result, while U.S. forces had a number of crack riflemen, they possessed few trained snipers at the beginning of the Vietnam involvement. The Viet Cong soldier considered himself relatively safe at ranges of 600 yards or more. There were instances of VC walking in plain sight at distances of 700 to 1,000 yards while they directed mortar fire on American positions. In the jungles and hamlets of the countryside, communists felt free to move about at will, confident they could spot U.S. patrols first and either avoid them or lure them into ambushes for their own marksmen.

So desperate was the need for qualified U.S. snipers to counteract the enemy in this new kind of war that when the Marines became the first U.S. forces in Vietnam to establish authentic sniper schools in midwinter 1965, sniper classes were only three days long, reminiscent of "schools" set up behind lines in Korea. With time, however, the "shooting classes" became true schools teaching not only marksmanship but also the other skills of the sniper's trade.

The schools set up in Vietnam were commanded by men like Captain Bob Russell and Captain James Land, men who were expert riflemen themselves and who fought for the sniper program to be permanently designated as a separate Military Occupational Specialty (MOS) that would carry over into peacetime training. As instructors, the commanders selected men like: Sergeant Carlos Hathcock, a Wimbledon Cup winner and Marine rifle champion, who went on to become the most successful sniper in history; Master Sergeant George Hurt, who at forty-two was the oldest of the sniper instructors, and a distinguished rifle and pistol marksman for more than seventeen years; Master Sergeant Donald L. Reinke, who first learned his craft in the field, then taught it; and Sergeant Donald G. Barker, who said he had won so many marksmanship awards he couldn't remember them all, and who became the first Marine in Vietnam to register a sniper kill.

The first schools were supplied with Winchesters and scopes pulled directly off the racks of sporting goods stores and military post exchanges. The targets were tin cans or C-rat boxes, whatever the instructors could find. While volunteers were supposed to be hand-picked combat veterans and expert riflemen, they were often haphazardly selected by commanders who did not understand the worth of the single shot fired with accuracy.

However, any doubts commanders had about snipers soon vanished. Schools cropped up on hills and "rear" areas throughout the Republic of Vietnam. Every Marine and Army regiment, often even down to battalion level, developed its own sniper program. Trained as riflemen, scouts, and hunters, snipers blanketed themselves across Vietnam. United States long-range sharpshooting promptly curtailed the VCs freedom of movement on the battlefield. "Old Charlie" was no longer safe. His brashness disappeared. North Vietnamese Army regulars came to fear so much the deadly crack of the hidden rifle that they offered large bounties for the heads of selected Marine and Army snipers. The bounty on Carlos Hathcock's head was three years' pay.

Although rarely publicized, the exploits of American Vietnam snipers have become a permanent part of the history of that war. Word of their feats spread quickly in-country. As:

Thirty-three guerrillas filtered onto a road that went past a sprawling Vietnamese cemetery. They were operating in their own backyard. This was "Charlie Land." "Mr. Charles" controlled it so thoroughly that he could afford to relax. None of the guerrillas showed concern as they sloppily formed up to march up the road to a village where they would replenish their food supplies.

Suddenly, the point man grabbed his chest as a bullet from a hidden rifleman sent him sprawling to the ground. The crack of the rifle eight hundred yards away was barely discernible. Hidden in tall knife grass, the U.S. Marine who fired the shot quickly jacked a fresh round into the still-smoking chamber of his Winchester Model 70. Off to his right, his teammate dropped a second VC. Within the next few minutes the pair of sharpshooting Marine snipers killed eleven Viet Cong and wounded six more as they rained lead into the panicked guerrilla ranks. Entire battalion operations and week-long sweeps rarely accounted for that many enemy casualties.

Farther north where the Fourth Marines sniper platoon operated only a few miles away from the Laotian border and the DMZ, an officer leading a patrol surprised a black-pajamaed figure who jumped into a boat and began paddling furiously downstream.

The officer snapped at his interpretor: "Tell that man to stop and come ashore."

The fleeting Vietnamese ignored the order.

"Sniper up!" barked the officer.

A young corporal dropped to the prone on the grass next to the officer. He sighted through his rifle scope, waiting.

"Put one across his bow," the officer ordered.

The bullet geysered the water a few feet ahead of the boat. The Vietnamese paddled faster.

"Put one *in* the boat."

The sniper's rifle barked again. The bullet ripped completely through the boat just above the water line and a foot forward of the paddler. That only made the Vietnamese work harder, convincing the officer that this fleeing man was no harmless fisherman.

"Kill him."

Coolly, without question, the corporal directed his final shot through the back of the VC's neck, knocking him dead into the water. The boat contained weapons. The Marine sniper had put every shot directly where his officer told him.

North of Chu Lai, a Marine patrol sweeping through a village on the peninsula called Old Snaggletooth stationed a two-man sniper team behind the village to catch Charlie leaving by the back door. One of these snipers was 19-year-old Lance Corporal R. D. Bundy. This was his first mission as a sniper.

"We could see Marines sweeping into the front of the village," Bundy recalled. He had been shooting large-bore rifles since he was nine. "At the same time our men were going in, armed Charlies were coming out the back."

Bundy spotted two VC sentries crouched at the edge of the village covering their comrades' withdrawal. The range was greater than eight hundred yards. Bundy cross-haired one of them and fired.

"He didn't know what hit him. The second guard was trying to figure out what happened to his buddy when I dinged him too."

Minutes later, a third guerrilla burst out of the village and through the brush some five hundred yards to the hidden sniper's front, running as hard as he could with his rifle at port arms. Bundy brought him down, too, with one single accurate shot.

Killing men like that, one at a time, personally and

calculatedly while not in the heat of full combat, required what sniper commanders like Captains Land and Russell unabashedly called "special men." While acknowledging that these men were indeed special, commanders sometimes found it difficult to describe just what it was that made them special. As for the snipers, each had his own reason for volunteering for this, the most deadly game of all—the hunting of other armed men.

"It's a challenge," said Sergeant Don Barker, "to sneak up on Old Charlie in his own backyard and put a hurtin' on him. I like being a sniper."

"I was good at it," Sergeant Carlos Hathcock liked to say. "I was saving Marine lives."

"I wanted to even the score," explained Marine Corporal Ronald A. Szpond, who had had buddies killed by the VC and who had himself been previously wounded in a booby trap explosion. "I wondered how I could get back at them. When I heard division wanted volunteers for the sniper school, I raised my hand because I think I'm a pretty good shot."

As soon as Szpond graduated from sniper school, he killed one VC and wounded another.

"I'm even for me," he said. "Now, I've got three buddies to settle things for."

Lance Corporal R. D. Bundy tallied nine enemy dead and four wounded in just a few weeks. For him, it was merely something "someone had to do."

Each "hunt" did not necessarily produce a kill. Sometimes a sniper waited for hours, even days, without getting off a single shot. But that shot rarely missed when it finally came. It was the cheapest and most effective way to kill the enemy.

"I figure that I accomplished the same thing with a thirteen-cent round that a B-52 loaded with bombs did," boasted one sniper, not without justification.

CHAPTER TWELVE

U.S. Marine Corporal
Gary Edwards
Vietnam, 1965

They called me "Hillbilly." I was a Tennessee mountain boy and the first man in my county to join the Marines during the Vietnam War. I was proud of that. I was a fighter. I was lean and lanky and my pa used to say I could whip a razorback boar one-on-one. Hillbilly boys were raised like that.

I strapped myself into the webbing of a C-130 Hercules for the flight from Okinawa to Phu Bai in the Republic of Vietnam. There was a bunch of other Marines on the plane, replacements like me. It was June and I was going to the Fourth Marines that had just landed in Vietnam in February. The other boys were awful quiet on the way over. They looked like if you said "Boo!" to one, you'd have a runaway on your hands.

"You boys ever do any talkin'?" I asked.

Two or three wouldn't even look at me. They pulled in their necks like a snapping turtle will that has his own considerations and doesn't want to be bothered. But this one kid facing me in the opposite row of webbing kind of looked me up and down.

"You talk?" I asked him.

"Does a bear shit in the woods?" he said.

He had that accent.

"You a mountain boy, huh?" I asked.

"Kentucky."

"Kentucky, huh? I'm from Tennessee. What's us mountain boys doin' over here in this shithole of the world?"

"LBJ say we gonna kick some ass."

"Well, I been known to do that before."

Phu Bai was a small airfield on the lowlands surrounded by distant mountains. I'd rather have been in the mountains; I felt exposed sitting out there in the middle of rice paddies. Besides, the U.S. hadn't been here long enough to do much to the base. It was just an Army communications outfit in quonsets and some rows of squad tents for the Fourth Marines. Most of the time chow consisted of C-rats which the cooks mixed together sometimes and heated. The only beer they had there was "33" and "Tiger Piss." That shit was worse than any moonshine or home brew.

"Shi—it!" said this one black guy in disgust as the aircraft ramp went down and we got our first on-the-ground look at Vietnam. The crew chief said we'd taken two bullet holes on our way in.

"Shi—it. Them little yellow motherfuckers don't want us here, we'll go *home*."

The sun was as hard and as bright as it was off a new sheet iron hay barn. We shouldered our sea bags and filed down the loading skids and onto the hot tarmac. The oil was melting out of it and stuck to your feet. The full blast of that 130-degree heat struck me like out of an open oven. I took one look around.

Sweat popped out all over my body—and down I went, flat on my ass.

"Shi—it," said the black guy. "Shi—it!"

The first sergeant asked for volunteers to go to the air wing as helicopter door gunners. I had been a grunt pounding the ground long enough. I wanted to ride for a change, so I volunteered. He didn't pick me for that.

Then he wanted men to transfer over to the heavy weapons section in Headquarters and Service Company. That seemed better than beating the bush. I got put in flame throwers. I didn't know much about that job, so I got transferred to 60-millimeter mortars.

One night a patrol out in the bush patrolling the perimeter got into some stuff and needed fire support. This lance corporal working with me had been doing mortars all along. He was good at it. We got the fire mission out, but it bothered me that I didn't know what I was doing. I kept thinking, *what if that lance hadn't been with me? The boys in the bush would have been hurting*.

I went to the first sergeant.

"First Sergeant, I don't know nothin' about mortars either," I admitted. "All I ever been since I was seventeen years old and come in this outfit is a grunt beatin' the bushes."

This time, like I figured, the first sergeant found a job for me I could do—squad leader beating the bush. I was a grunt, and grunt I was destined to be. We went out for days at a time on LRRPs (long range recon patrols). After one ten-day patrol, we came back in on stand-down. The Right Guide, or Assistant Platoon Sergeant, came around and told me not to even bother washing my dirty ass, but to report to company office immediately. I thought I was either going back out or something bad had happened at home. I trotted across the tarmac aircraft apron and ducked into the first sergeant's tent. He looked up and grinned at me.

"Edwards, we found something you can do," he said.

I looked at him. Was he making fun of me or something?

"You've been selected to go to sniper school to become part of the new sniper team. Twenty men in the division are going."

I qualified Expert in boot camp with a score of 228 out of a possible 250. The only other man to outshoot me, with a 230, was a *yankee*.

I flew to Da Nang the next morning. This was September. Twenty of us from division went through five days of training under Captain Bob Russell, Gunnery Sergeant George Hurt, and Staff Sergeant Donald Barker. At the end of the week, they issued each of us a Winchester Model 70 30.06 bolt-action rifle with a Unertl scope and one box of Camp Perry match ammunition.

"Here's twenty rounds each," Gunny Hurt said. "I want twenty kills. *One shot—one kill.*"

That was what he told us.

A black sergeant named Brown was in charge of the three snipers at Phu Bai. He was a skinny guy. The other sniper besides me was tall and skinny too. Kentucky was a lance corporal from Kentucky. Where else? We didn't have a spotter or observer, which didn't matter anyhow because company didn't know what to do with us. The first thing that happened when we got off the plane again ready to go out and ding Chucks with our new hunting rifles was that we got stuck standing perimeter sentry duty.

"Looky here, First Sergeant," I protested. "What can we do with a bolt-action rifle if they do hit us?"

"Quit your bitching, Hillbilly, and pull your duty."

I pulled my duty. I bitched, but I pulled it. After that, all three of us, every sniper at Phu Bai, got moved over to some 155-millimeter howitzer batteries and we walked a sentry line there for awhile. Guarding a perimeter. With *sniper rifles*.

We bitched so much about that, that we finally started going out into the bush with the platoons, but it was the same old shit in a different place. We set up PPBs—Platoon Patrol Bases—out on the flats among the pines. We held up during the day and ran night ambushes and patrols. I couldn't believe it. For all the good scoped rifles did us in operations like that, we might as well have been carrying clubs. We tried to explain to the platoon leaders that we were *snipers*. We shot gooks from a *distance*.

I told Sergeant Brown to get in touch with Captain Russell over at the sniper school and explain to *him* what they were doing with us. I don't know if he did or not, but when we returned to Phu Bai after one of our PPB operations, an officer from battalion recon was waiting for us.

"We have a mission for you three," he said.

"We are good at standing perimeter duty, sir," Kentucky said.

The sarcasm didn't miss the recon officer. He grinned.

"No. This is a *real* mission," he said. "Sniping."

"Finally?"

"Hallelujah!" Kentucky hooted.

Sergeant Brown shook his head. "We had bolt-action rifles going on patrol. They'll probably give us .45 pistols to go sniping with."

Battalion gave the mission briefing.

"You're going into Charlie country," a sergeant said. "It's never been worked before by anybody. Anything in the area is open game. You can kill anything you see in there—providing you make sure they're carrying weapons."

The three of us were going to work as a group, escorted into Indian Country by a rifle squad armed with M-14s, an M-60 machine gun, and an M-79 grenade launcher. We didn't complain though. It was still a mission.

An H-34 chopper flew us in over flats so thick with jungle it looked like dog fur. The chopper slicked into a grassy clearing snuggled up next to a river that resembled a muddy road. A few tin-roofed buildings marked an ARVN outpost. A Vietnamese tee-wee, a lieutenant, came out to meet the heavily armed squad unassing the helicopter. He spoke good English, but he did not seem too happy to see us.

"This is VC country," he said. "We don't bother them—and they don't bother us."

He cleared his throat and looked unhappy. "Until *now*," he added.

Nevertheless, early the next morning when the sun was still only a threat, he guided us out to the back side of a hill. We got down on our hands and knees and crawled through the tall grass to the crest and peeked over to where the early morning bathed the valley below in pale light. The tee-wee pointed out a trail. It emerged from the jungle on the right and worked its way through knife grass and other patches of jungle to the edge of a Buddhist temple studded with spires and crowded with stone carvings. It continued from there through shorter grass to a distant village whose hootches were scattered among bamboo and palms.

The tee-wee said, "Every morning about nine-thirty, VC walk on that trail. They go to the village. They walk through the village like they own it."

"We can put a stop to that good shit," Kentucky said. He looked excited. The tee-wee looked nervous.

We quickly thinned out some of the tall grass to make fields of fire. Brown, Kentucky, and I arranged ourselves side by side on the hilltop overlooking the trail where it first emerged from the jungle into the clearing. The rest of the squad hid themselves in the grass on either flank where they could provide covering fire for us if it came to that. The operation looked disorganized, more like a cluster fuck than anything else, but we confidently settled in to wait the appearance of a target.

It was better than hunting deer in the Smoky Mountains.

I just happened to glance at my watch—it was 9:05—when a group of five VC wearing black pajamas emerged from the forest, following the trail to the village. They weren't visible when I dropped my eyes to my wrist, but there they were when I looked up again, filling my scope with the biggest and most dangerous game I had ever hunted.

They acted very casual coming out of the morning shadows. Obviously they felt safe. The leader had his AK-47 slung across his back, one carried an M-1 carbine at sling arms, the third was using a bolt-action Chinese rifle as a walking stick. The last two were equally unconcerned.

I had been designated to take the first shot on the point man, while Brown and Kentucky immediately followed suit on the next two in line. I lined up my man in my cross hairs. We estimated the range at close to one thousand yards; later, we paced it off, and that was how far it was. The first thing I noticed through the scope was the man's face. It was a young, healthy face. He was laughing and saying something to the man in the file behind him.

119

I don't know how to describe how I felt, but I wasn't scared. This was what I had trained for. It was different than in a firefight when everybody was burning ammo and you never knew who hit what. I was deliberately taking my time and lining up on a human target. When he fell—and I knew he would—there could never be any doubt that it was my bullet that killed him.

But I didn't think about that. I thought about the mechanics of it. Cross hairs. Breathing. Smooth trigger squeeze.

I shot.

Brown and Kentucky cracked their rifles a split second later, so that the reports sounded like one instead of several distinct ones. Three enemy soldiers, my smiling one and the next two behind him, crumpled in the trail like bags of old dirty laundry dumped out of the back of a six-by truck. After an instant's shocked reaction, the two surviving VC wheeled like they'd been goosed by a two-by-four and bolted back toward the jungle. The M-60 machine gun on our flank opened up and chewed up terrain all around them, but they escaped.

The event made *Stars And Stripes* as the first recorded kill by a Marine sniper unit in Vietnam. It wasn't though. Sergeant Barker made the first kill just a few months before when he and Captain Russell and Gunny Hart were setting up the school. I'm sure, however, that we were the school's first students to get kills.

The face of the first man I shot has always stuck with me. I can still see his gold tooth. He wore black pajamas and rubber tire sandals and had a bag of rice tied around his waist. Another of the dead had a Chinese canteen; I took it for a souvenir.

We radioed for a chopper and loaded the bodies

onto it. The tee-wee looked more unhappy than ever. When we delivered the body count to Phu Bai, they were confirmed and then thrown into a big horseshoe trench dug by a bulldozer. The bulldozer pushed in just enough dirt to cover them. The next corpses brought in would be dumped on top of that and covered and then the next and so on like that until the trench was full.

When people asked me what it was like to kill a man, I said, "You'd have to do it to know."

Maybe I couldn't use a flame thrower or send out a mortar fire mission, but I could shoot. We thought after we proved ourselves as snipers that things would be different at Phu Bai, but they weren't. It was the same old shit again of going out ten or fifteen days at a time on the PPBs. All three of us snipers—Brown, Kentucky, and me—usually traveled together. We never had a spotter or observer. We were the first school Captain Russell put out. We were still learning and the units were still learning how to use us.

On a hilltop not far from Phu Bai the Marines had set up a communications outpost to relay artillery fire requests back to the batteries. There were some smaller tents and a big platoon GP surrounded by concertina and booby traps. Every morning about nine, a VC came out of the wood line below and fired a burst up the hill in the direction of the platoon tent. He punched a few holes in the tents and kicked up some dirt, but otherwise he hadn't hit anything. Still, after awhile, the men got tired of the VC's peculiar form of reveille. They wanted something done about him.

"Send us a sniper."

Brown, Kentucky, and I choppered out to the hill and set up in cover on a ridge top with a spotting scope we managed to check out of special services.

121

You could have set your watch by the VC's arrival. It was like his wife came in every morning: "Wake up, wake up, Nguyen. It's time to go shoot at the Americans." Right at 9 A.M. Charlie ripped off his rounds from the bush with a PpSH submachine gun, Chinese made, and then hightailed it home to work his water buffalo.

That was all right.

"We'll have his orange juice ready for him tomorrow morning," Sergeant Brown promised.

Just as expected, Charlie VC came back the next morning. We were waiting on the ridge. It was *too* easy. The VC was only about eighteen or nineteen years old. A scrawny kid with a mop of black hair. Just as he stood up in the bushes, aimed up the hill, and fired his first burst, Sergeant Brown sighted in on him. "So long, motherfucker." He fired. The range was only about two hundred fifty yards. Brown's bullet blew out the VC's throat.

We made a few more kills like that—VC walking down a trail or something. They never knew what hit them. I still remember the first one with the gold tooth, and there was one other that really bothered me. It wasn't a sniper kill. I was grunting it at the time, like we did when we weren't being used as snipers. I had traded my Winchester for a M-14. My company was working its way up toward Hue, sweeping this ville that was supposed to be headquarters for an estimated company of hardcore.

Marines surrounded the village. A spotter plane flew in low over the hootches, its loudspeakers blaring in Vietnamese, warning the villagers to come out while they could. We knew they were in there, burrowed into bunkers and spider holes. But nobody came out.

We waited. Finally, the CO called for a napalm strike. Napalm works like if you strike a match to a house filled with gas fumes. Only, it has this Styrofoam in it or something that sticks to everything while it burns. GIs used to sing a song about it: *Napalm sticks to kids*.

Jets came screaming over just above treetop level and the napalm came tumbling out in strings. It made an enormous gaseous explosion that flamed up like a volcano. Spine-shattering screaming and hollering came from the flames. It was hard to tell the difference between people and live pigs cooking.

We watched. Nothing could have lived through that. When the fires burned down, the Marines ringing the village stood and started to move in. Gunfire erupted from the ashes. A bullet almost tore the arm off the guy next to me. He dropped to the ground screaming. He tried to grab his wildly flopping arm and hold it. Another Marine took a hit in the gut. He doubled over before he sat down hard in a rice paddy and started yelling for a corpsman. I dived behind a dike and, like a gopher chased by a cat, started digging in with my belly and toes and fingers, with every piece of my anatomy that could move.

The CO called for artillery this time. The shelling destroyed what the napalm hadn't burned. Little remained of the village except a big pile of ashes studded with the stumps of shattered palms. We stood up again and advanced on line. My squad swept around on the right flank. Our feet puffed up little clouds of ashes. We avoided the shell craters. A singed pig with the glistening white of its exposed ribs showing lumbered by with ear-piercing squeals. All around us was nothing but smoldering hootches and some dead roasted pigs and dead chickens with their feathers burned off.

Underneath, the village must have been honeycombed with tunnels. Destroying the hootches revealed numerous bunkers and openings. One of the guys heard noises coming from one. We surrounded it and I dropped a teargas grenade into the opening. Something let out a terrifying squall. My hair stood on end. When a black cat came tearing out of the hole, every hair stuck out like a porcupine quill, and in its excitement mistook my leg for the nearest tree, we damned near killed each other before things got straightened out.

We lined out on the next bunker. Noises came from that one too.

"Watch out, boys. If it's another cat, Hillbilly'll run away on us."

A draftee named Danny stood about fifteen yards to the rear with an M-60 machine gun on a strap across his shoulder trained directly on the bunker opening. He stood there and watched, ready, while a sergeant tossed a frag grenade into the bunker.

The grenade detonated underground. The ground seemed to rise an inch or so and then settle in a cloud of dust and ashes. Dust surged out of the bunker door.

After the smoke settled, a tunnel rat crept inside and dragged out the body of a wizened old woman whose bones rattled like a rice straw mattress. She was torn all to pieces; her left eye had been blown out. The grenade must have landed in her lap.

The tunnel rat ventured inside again and came out with a dead boy of about eighteen and an AK-47. He said that was all of them. What we didn't know at the time was that the bunker contained a rear entrance that opened behind a stand of fire-scorched bamboo over to our right. I happened to glance up just as a pregnant woman clambered from it and charged silently out of the bamboo toward the nearest GI, the machine gunner Danny.

My eyes took in everything about her in a split instant. She was a tiny woman, like most Vietnamese, with her huge belly stuck out and stretching against this old black smock-dress thing she wore. She must have been about ready to foal. Her eyes were wild and fierce with the whites showing, like the eyes of coyotes I've seen trapped by dogs back in Tennessee. She didn't utter a sound. She just came at Danny with an upraised ice pick in her tiny fist.

"Danny! Look out!"

Danny froze, staring at her.

I had my M-14 on automatic. Instinct swung it up and around for me. She was two steps away from sinking her ice pick into Danny's chest when I cut her almost in half. She burst like when you split a watermelon. Her exploding pregnant part sprayed the squad with blood and gore and pieces of unborn baby. Then the two halves of her collapsed on the ground and twitched grotesquely. We found out that her tongue had been cut out. We never found out why though. Maybe the VC had done it for cooperating with the Americans. Maybe her charge with the ice pick was her desperate way of showing the VC that she no longer cooperated with the Americans and didn't have to have her nose or ears cut off too.

Killing a pregnant woman always stuck with me, just like the face of the first man I killed on the trail. I can still see her belly and the ice pick, and I can still see that gold tooth.

CHAPTER THIRTEEN

U.S. Marine Lance Corporal Craig Roberts Vietnam, 1965

Sal and I hunted night after night. We hunted—and we waited on a stand. We drew an area of operations with the First Marine Division across the Yen River near Hill 22. Our job was to go out on night patrols and stay behind to zap dinks we caught sneaking back to their holes at dawn. That was the way the gooks had been operating against us. It seemed like a good thing to turn the tables on them.

Nothing happened most of the time. We dropped off from a patrol, just this Chicano, Sal Rodriguez, from East Los Angeles and me and the rifle and a grunt for rear security. We set up somewhere in a hide and waited for dawn and the VC. At first light we watched farmers pass in the distance with their water buffalo, or old women chewing betel nut with baskets suspended on poles across their shoulders, walking stoically in the fresh sunlight.

It seemed 90 percent of war was nothing but waiting

for something to happen. I hated the waiting. Time dragged, and the dragging gave you too much time to think.

It was a bonus and a few minutes of excitement, exactly like a big game hunt, whenever we spotted VC sneaking back from their night's mischief. Suddenly, we reversed roles with them. Instead of the hunted, *we* became the hunters hidden in the jungle like ghosts, who killed unseen and then vanished into the bamboo.

Killing like that was personal, not like in a firefight when it was hard to tell who killed who. Through the scope you saw the expressions on their faces in that instant before you sent a bullet screaming into their flesh. Mostly, they were young faces, some no older than sixteen. I was just nineteen, so their youth had little impact. I killed a few, Sal killed some, and if there was any feeling to it after the first one or two, it was satisfaction. We were doing something personal to avenge Marines who had been killed and maimed by mines, booby traps, and gook snipers.

Going to the enemy on his own turf and killing him was better than waiting until he came on yours. We slept during the days and with the fall of night we packed up our rifle and scope, like a shift worker packing a lunch, and went to work. It was a job. Like Sal quipped, it kept us busy and off the street corners. Sal grew up in the barrios of Los Angeles and knew about street corners.

"I've shot at more splibs (the Marine word for *blacks*) in L.A. than I have gooks over here," he complained after one disappointing night's work.

The sniper rifles we used were big game rifles right off the rack from some sporting goods store—30.06 Model 70 Winchesters, bolt action, some with Unertl scopes, others with any scopes we could get. They were good for long fields of fire, out to around one thousand meters. At shorter ranges, a standard M-14 worked just as well. In fact, the M-14 worked even better with running targets since the target kept running out of the field of view of some scopes and was hard to follow. Half of the rice field shots we made in the Da Nang enclave could have been made better with the open sights on an M-14.

One night, a Marine patrol dropped us off and we set up on a large mound of dirt that looked like a scaled-down replica of the Rock of Gibraltar. It was about twenty-five meters high with steep sides and just enough room at the top for two men to hide prone in a tuft of grass. Sal and I scrambled to the top while our security rifleman, who wasn't too happy out here all night with just the three of us, established himself at the base in the knife grass to protect our rear.

I clamped a pair of M-14 bipods to the barrel of the Winchester, extended the legs, chopped some grass to hide the weapon's silhouette, all this in silence, and then rolled over on my back and lay staring at the stars with Sal, each of us caught up in our own thoughts as we waited for dawn and the VC to start moving back to their spider traps and tunnels to hide for the day.

Time dragged. I thought about Rita and felt a burst of jealousy that almost made me sit straight up at the thought of some stateside Jodie watching the stars with her while I was stuck over here in this shithole.

I forced myself to stop thinking. It was hard, but you had to do it.

The sun rose slowly. First, there were long shadows. Rice fields emerged out of the shadows like green squares gridded by dikes. The rains came more infrequently nearing the end of the monsoon season, and it was already hot. It hadn't cooled off much during the night, and there was no breeze. It was time for Charlie to be coming home. Sal scanned the fields for me, then put down the binoculars and wiped sweat out of his eyes with his sleeve.

Suddenly, he stared, snatched up the glasses again, and locked onto something. He sank closer to the ground.

"Check this shit out," he murmured, exhaling slowly. I gently pushed the grass away from the rifle to get to the scope.

"Seven hundred meters at two o'clock," Sal said.

I snugged the butt stock against my shoulder to get the best picture from the scope. A dike and a line of jungle lunged at me through the lenses. I scanned, slowly, until I picked up the first gook. I went down the line, counting them—*seven* gooks walking along a dike toward the Tuy Loan River like they were out for their morning constitutional. It surprised me to find such a large group. Usually, at that time of the morning, they came in twos and threes at the most.

We had strict orders not to fire unless we saw weapons. There were no "free fire zones" as there were later in the war. No problem with this bunch though.

"Okay. I see weapons. I'm going for Tailend Charlie."

I had read this book once about an American sniper in World War II who always picked off the last man in a column so he wouldn't spook the others until he could get off another shot or two. Now seemed the time to try it out.

I laid cross hairs at the top of the last man's head, anticipating bullet drop at this range. The man was young and bareheaded with an SKS thrown over one shoulder. His skin glowed almost red in the morning sunlight, like an Indian's. He looked tired.

He turned his head and stared almost directly into my eyes. I knew he could not possibly see me, but it was a bit unnerving nonetheless, looking eye to eye like that through the scope with a man I was about to kill.

I adjusted my eye to the scope. If you held your eye too far back, the field through the scope diminished, too near and the recoil drove the scope into your eyebrow. I could almost hear the coach at the firing range saying:

"Squeeze the trigger like you squeeze a woman's nipple."

I took up trigger slack—and fired.

So long, shitbird.

An invisible fist slammed out of the sky and knocked the dink off the dike into the rice paddy. He splashed frantically about like a wounded duck, alerting the others who had not heard the shot. Two of them immediately jumped into the rice to rescue their comrade. The others bolted along the dike toward a tree line by the river.

"Watch your breathing," Sal advised. "Your muzzle is rising and falling."

I clenched my breath inside my teeth. I tasted sweat. Sweat blurred my vision through the scope. I blinked and the two gooks dragging the wounded one through the rice water came clear, like a TV picture suddenly in focus. I fired again. A little spout of water erupted in front of them. Sal was watching through the field glasses.

"Too much lead on him!" he exclaimed. "Roberts, nail the fuckheads. They're getting away!"

The VC left a wake of water behind them as they dragged their wounded friend, they were moving so fast. Each VC had the downed one clamped by an arm. He looked badly hurt. His head lolled forward and down into the water. If my bullet hadn't killed him, then they'd likely finish him off by drowning.

Why didn't they just drop him and save their own asses?

"Give 'em hell!" Sal cried in exasperation.

I squeezed off again. One of the dinks stumbled and grabbed himself—but he kept going. Why was it you could shoot these little bastards with an elephant gun and they'd still get up and run off? An American would die from a little piece of shrapnel you could hardly see.

Sal was no longer calm.

"They're getting away!" he screamed, forgetting himself in his excitement. "Fuck it. I'm gonna open up too. At least we can scare the shit out of 'em."

That brought the private from below scrambling up the Rock of Gibraltar to get in his licks. Sal rose to one knee to aim his M-14. The three of us firing made geysers in the water all around the fleeing VC. Each time I fired, the recoil jarred me off target. I wasted time getting back on. The Winchester needed to be heavier with a heavier barrel. These were things they corrected later in the war.

The VC reached the bamboo thicket by the river and faded from sight. It was abruptly peaceful again in the morning sunlight with the rice gridded off into green squares and some birds calling from the trees behind us.

One thing you didn't do when there was just three of you was wait around after the action. We slid quickly from our perch and headed for the escape route we had already picked out, cautious now lest the tables turned again and *we* once again became the hunted.

CHAPTER FOURTEEN

Even though history reveals that it is the soldier who can shoot who plays the most important role in battlefield victory, American GIs have progressively become poorer marksmen. Except for snipers and a few hard-core Army Regulars and Marines, U.S. soldiers of this century have rarely attained any true skill or proficiency with their weapons.

During World War I, the American soldier expended an average of 7,000 rounds for each enemy casualty. The average jumped to 25,000 during World War II, while Korea doubled that figure to 50,000 rounds. Estimates range anywhere from 200,000 to 400,000 rounds fired for each enemy body count in Vietnam.

In 1971 when Major Lones Wigger, Jr., assumed command of the U.S. Army's Twenty-third Infantry Division's Sniper School in Vietnam, his duties included marksmanship training for the division's replacement troops.

Wigger was an expert rifleman. His marksmanship earned him a spot on the 1968 U.S. Olympic rifle team that competed in Mexico City. Although he won no medals at the Olympics, he took a silver medal in the three hundred meter prone and a bronze in small-bore free rifle two years later during the World Championships. He was also a member of three gold medal winning teams and six silver medal winning teams at the World Championships. His 1971 tour in Vietnam was his second. In 1967, he served as an agricultural advisor for an infantry operations staff in Vietnam.

What Wigger discovered in Vietnam in 1971 stunned him.

"I found the average replacement could not hit a silhouette target at twenty-five meters, knew little of basic marksmanship fundamentals, and did not understand why he needed to zero his rifle."

Wigger was not the only one to make this discovery. Master Sergeant Emil W. Heugatter found the same thing in 1969 at Cu Chi when he took charge of the Twenty-fifth Infantry Division's Combat Marksmanship School, an euphemism for "sniper school" since the Army was still squeamish about admitting it was training snipers.

In testing the marksmanship proficiency of selected line platoons, Heugatter and Sergeant First Class Cleone L. Anthony placed one-foot-square targets on stakes at a distance of twenty-five meters from the firing line. Only about *ten percent* of the soldiers in the selected platoons were able to hit the targets. Some of the poor showing was due to lack of marksmanship knowledge, some because most of the soldiers did not understand why they should zero their rifles, nor how to do it, and some because of poor maintenance. The front sights of some rifles had rusted beyond adjustment, some had worn-out barrels, and one rifle had *no* front sights at all.

These findings extended even to officers and NCOs.

Vietnam, say many military observers, was the result of decades of military de-emphasis on marksmanship in favor of returning to the old philosophy of massed firepower that dates back to the stand-up-and-shoot armies of Europe. It is a proven fact that only a small percentage of soldiers in combat ever actually fire their weapons *at* the enemy.

"Only one out of five servicemen in Korea regularly fired their rifles in combat," observed Major General M. A. Edson. "This is due to lack of confidence based on insufficient training."

Whatever the cause, even those soldiers who *were* firing *at* the enemy were not hitting him. Lack of marksmanship training and the philosophy of mass firepower accounted for the wild spraying of bullets with the automatic M-16 that characterized much of the fighting in Vietnam, and for the fact that many soldiers did not fire their weapons at all except in general ineffective bursts. That was why it took 200,000 to 400,000 rounds to obtain a single enemy casualty.

"The marksmanship ability of the average soldier has deteriorated so badly that we would be hard pressed to win a conventional war," said Lones Wigger, Jr., now a lieutenant colonel and Director of the U.S. Shooting Team. "We are fooling ourselves if we believe the American soldier can shoot."

Currently, hundreds of officers and enlisted men fill marksmanship-related jobs throughout the Army. There are at least 3,000 other assignments requiring shooting proficiency. Nearly 1,700 ROTC shooting teams require coaches. In addition to all this, marksmen are needed to teach basic combat training and advanced infantry training. Marksmen fill positions on weapons committees and post range control organizations. They are on staff assignments at all levels of command, including the Department of the Army.

Yet, marksmanship continues to decline.

"Two major obstacles must be surmounted if military marksmanship is to be saved," said Colonel Wigger. "The first is bureaucratic resistance to change. The second is the fact that most Army officers and NCOs think they know rifle marksmanship. They do not know that they do not know."

In 1956, the Army introduced the *Trainfire* system of marksmanship. This system, depending upon lessons learned in Korea, drew away from basic sharpshooting techniques in favor of simulated combat conditions. Instead of forming a fundamental base for accurate shooting, Trainfire stressed cover and concealment with man-sized *pop-up* targets appearing at various ranges. Soldiers were expected to snap-shoot in combat before they had learned the proper steps to hitting *known-distance* targets, resulting in loss of accuracy. Known-distance shooting was de-emphasized and eventually phased out.

The problem was compounded in the 1960s when the Army adopted the *quick kill* training policy and the rapid-firing M-16. Designed for close-in fighting, the M-16 was capable of fully automatic fire. It used smaller cartridges, which meant more ammunition could be carried and expended. *Quick kill*, as the term implies, called for rapid point shooting at targets. Aimed fire was seldom used. Volume automatic fire became the rule. Typically, soldiers sprayed bullets at the enemy in hopes that *some* of the rounds would hit him. More often than not, they *all* missed.

The men who trained snipers for Vietnam—Major Dick Culver, Captain Jim Land, Captain Bob Russell, Lieutenant Colonel Lones Wigger, Jr., and all the others—stressed known-distance shooting over Trainfire and quick kill. Trainfire, they argued, did not allow the soldier to know where his shots were going; therefore, he failed to acquire confidence in his rifle and enthusiasm for shooting. While combat conditions were emphasized in the training, the training was failing to make combat shooters out of soldiers.

Known-distance shooting, on the other hand, started with the fundamentals of shooting. It developed good habits in aiming, sight alignment, breathing, trigger control, and follow-through. It formed good shooting habits in the soldier and helped him retain them. This type of training led to the *probability* of a hit in combat, whereas snap-shooting, spraying, and fire volume assured only the *possibility* of a hit.

"We also need to re-emphasize the sniper rifle," Wigger said. "It once again proved its usefulness in Vietnam. Because of the short maximum effective range of the M-16, we are developing an environment for sniper employment. The long-range effectiveness of the sniper rifle complements the short range of the M-16. An enemy would have difficulty taking advantage of the short range of the M-16 if the sniper and his rifle were effectively employed."

According to Wigger, no more than three hundred experienced rifle shooters remain on active duty in the U.S. Army. These numbers are dwindling rapidly due to retirement of former snipers and sharpshooters, an Army training program that stresses mass firepower over accurate shooting, and the dying out of competitive marksmanship.

"Few new shooters are entering the system," Wigger said. "When competitive shooting dies, our instructor expertise in marksmanship will die with it."

That the marksmanship program based on principles of known-distance shooting *worked* was demonstrated repeatedly in Vietnam.

Major John R. Foster, Wigger's counterpart for the 101st Airborne Division, started a marksmanship refresher program during which combat companies sent in two men each week for training. Foster conducted a little demonstration to point out the value of marksmanship fundamentals. When each weekly contingent of about thirty seasoned combat troops arrived, he had them select from among themselves the worst marksman of the group, usually a "Gomer Pyle" type. Then, while the rest of the class went through an introductory briefing, instructors force-fed Gomer Pyle basic marksmanship.

Afterwards, each man of the group, except Gomer, stepped to the firing line with his M-16 and two fully loaded thirty-round magazines. The target was a single man-sized silhouette placed fifty meters downrange. The shooter was instructed to fire as many rounds as he could within a one-minute time limit. His position and rate of fire was left up to him.

Most of the soldiers shot from a standing position on full automatic. Many didn't even bother to use their rear sights. The group averaged four to six hits *total* out of approximately eighteen hundred rounds of ammunition expended.

Then Gomer Pyle, selected because he was considered the worst shot of the group, stepped to the firing line. Unlike the others, he had received a simple five-minute class on fundamentals and was required to fire in the prone and only from the semi-automatic position. Invariably, Gomer hit the target more times with his controlled fire of 60 rounds than did the rest of the group with its mass firepower of 1,800 rounds.

"Do I make my point?" Major Foster asked, stepping to the front after the demonstration ended. "One accurate shot fired with deliberate precision is worth more than a hundred fired without control."

Major Wigger personally selected his sniper instructors from competitive marksmen who knew the fundamentals of shooting and how to teach them. Sniper candidates, previously trained in Trainfire and quick kill, adept at mass fire tactics, expressed skepticism when Wigger stood up in front of them and promised: "Within a week you will, ninety percent of the time, be getting first-round hits on man-sized targets at six hundred meters."

And they *were*.

In terms of body count and effect on the enemy's morale, snipers in Vietnam proved more combat effective than entire battalions. For example, snipers of the Army's Ninth Infantry Division working in the Mekong Delta from January to July 1969 accounted for 1,139 enemy KIAs.

No *battalion* in the division did so well.

CHAPTER FIFTEEN

U.S. Marine Sergeant Carlos Hathcock Vietnam, 1967

Near the mountain peak called Dong Den, twenty kilometers northwest of the Da Nang Air base, the Cade River serpentined its way down from the green mountains on its way to the South China Sea. It curved abruptly east across the flat bottom of a narrow, elbow-shaped valley the Americans called Elephant Valley from an action that occurred there one night in June 1965.

Infantrymen from the Third Marine Regiment were set up on the lower jungle-covered ridges of Dong Den when, incredibly enough, they heard through the darkness what they thought to be the trumpeting of *elephants*. They radioed in for artillery illumination rounds to bring the valley out of shadows. Sure enough, it *was* elephants. A string of eight of them with their drivers was wending its way across the flat rice land. The elephants were loaded with heavy cannon and ammunition for the Viet Cong.

Artillery made short work of the pachyderm convoy. The action went down in Marine lore as the Battle of Elephant Valley.

Since it was a natural gateway from the north to the south, the valley constantly swarmed with hamburgers on resupply and replacement missions. I thought it would make a productive area of operation for my sniper rifle. Johnny Burke and I laid it on with intel that we'd be in the valley and with artillery for cover fire if we needed it, then hitched a chopper ride off Hill 55 to join a squad on patrol toward the Cade River.

The two of us always traveled light. I carried a canvas bandoleer containing eighty-four match-grade 30.06 full-metal-jacketed rounds of ammo, two canteens, a Kabar combat knife, a .45 pistol, a compass and map, and a few of the smaller cans of C-ration peanut butter, jelly, cheese and crackers. Burke carried about the same. In addition, between us, we had the Winchester Model 70 with scope, an M-14 rifle, binoculars, a radio, and a high-powered spotting scope. As soon as we returned from one mission, we prepared our gear for the next so that we were always ready to go on a moment's notice.

As soon as the squad entered Elephant Valley, we slipped off from it, watched our back trail for a few minutes to make sure we hadn't been spotted and followed, then made our way around the hamlet of Truong Dinh to a thick tree line at the base of Dong Den. After first scouting out a quick escape route, just in case, we selected our hide, prepared natural camouflage, and burrowed into it just as the sun was going down and making a living Oriental postcard out of the valley. We were ready for whatever dawn brought in the way of hamburgers sneaking back to their lairs.

To our front stretched a broad expanse of open wet

rice fields. They were gridded off by low dikes into rough squares. One main dike, sticking up out of the water about two feet higher than the others, ran parallel to our position and served as a pathway across the rice land. It was about 700 meters from us. That was where we figured we'd get action. Beyond that dike was another 1,000 meters of open rice fields which finally abutted against a long, low line of bamboo and palms marking the site of the rice farmers' hootches. Behind the hootches flowed the Cade River—or the Ca De Song, as the Vietnamese called it.

As always, Burke and I set up in the bush and settled down to wait without a word passing. Voices carry, especially during the quiet times just before nightfall and at dawn. Burke simply nodded approval of our selection, I nodded back, and we settled down to let the warm night conceal us.

An occasional jet airplane streaked overhead and a distant artillery flare marked its smoky trail against the sky, just to let us know there was still a war going on. Otherwise, there was just the natural night sounds of insects and animals. Burke and I had learned to become a natural part of that night. Captain Jim Land sometimes laughed and said I smelled more like an animal in the jungle than like a man. That was part of the secret of what kept the hamburgers from claiming the white feather in my bush hat.

One of us catnapped while the other kept watch, but at dawn we were both awake and alert, waiting. Dawn brought the best hunting. We silently watched the gray light in the east creep down the river valley. When the sun rose, it brought a fine pink light that turned pastel the fog snuggled against the distant mountains. Then came the harsher shadows. The red sun shimmered off the rice pools—the young rice had not yet broken the surface—and there was a slight aliveness in the air promising another hellishly hot day in paradise. The white feather in my hat remained utterly motionless; it was so still you had to suck in the air as from a vacuum.

We heard them coming. Burke cast me a quizzical look. I shrugged. The noise got louder until it sounded like a dump truck full of empty tin cans driving across last year's cornfield.

Then, as we watched, a full company-sized element of NVA—about eighty men—came clanking into view from the direction of the Cade River. We expected the element to cut around opposite us through the distant tree line and on across the mountains. Instead, the hamburgers selected the dike path that led directly across the center of the rice fields. The path was narrow. They strung out along it like foolish geese where there wasn't any real cover or concealment for a thousand meters in any direction. They must have been in one hell of a hurry to take such chances in the open rather than climb the safer but slower route through the mountains.

I studied them through the binoculars while Burke used the spotting scope. They kept coming.

They were just kids. Boots. Uncle Ho's first new generation. Their khaki uniforms looked fresh. Their turtle-shaped helmets showed no dents or wear. Their Kalashnikov rifles gleamed with new oil in the morning sunshine. Obviously, they were green replacements on their way down from the north for their first taste of war. Even the officers and NCOs—who wore side-arms—must have had little combat experience to have led their command into the open in broad daylight. It was what GIs called a *cluster fuck*—moving right through the open within easy rifle range.

Burke's eyes widened. "Can you believe this shit?"

They were his first words since the day before.

I whispered back: "They look like Boy Scouts on their way to a jamboree."

Burke looked to me for a cue. Ordinarily, I wouldn't have thought of opening sniper fire on an element that large, especially not one of seasoned troops. That was why you had artillery on call. But these were untried soldiers, greenhorns. I kept thinking about it as the company clanked its way into the center of the rice field.

If we called in artillery, many of the NVA would get away and scatter into the jungles where Sparrowhawk, the Marine ready reaction force, would have to fly in and dig them out. Greenhorns or not, they were still capable of biting like bamboo vipers. Marines would get killed.

Maybe we could prevent that.

It was flat, easy shooting across the valley. There was no wind, no mist, no mirages to interfere with a sight picture.

The NVA column—rattling, clanking, chattering—reached the center of the shimmering rice fields.

I made up my mind.

"The hamburger with the pistol out front—I'll take him. You take the one in the rear."

The pounding of my pulse made the cross hairs rise and fall against the image of the officer at the head of the column. No matter how many times you do it, there is still that sense of excitement. I took a deep slow breath to calm my nerves.

I drilled the officer. Before the rifle report clapped against the face of Dong Den, Burke dropped a man carrying a pistol at the back of the formation. As we hoped, the rest of the NVA panicked. I managed to kill a recruit before the NVA scrambled for the only cover available—the back side of the dike. They plopped belly down in the stagnant rice pond and hugged the side of the dike. Just like frightened Boy Scouts. They were doing exactly what I wanted them to do. This was one time when panic might have been a good thing. If it had driven them in a mindless stampede for the distant tree line, most of them would have escaped.

Instead, I almost laughed at the confusion that huddled them together in the open like sheep.

I kept my scope trained on the dike. I knew the next few minutes would be busy ones. At least one or two would poke up their heads to see what was going on—prairie dogs out of their holes. I made their heads explode like pumpkins. Seeing his men die so terrified the only remaining officer that he jumped up blindly and bolted for the river. I followed him with my cross hairs. He hadn't gone more than a few churning steps through the knee-deep water before I dropped him.

Within three minutes after my first shot, six of the enemy lay dead. Now leaderless and without the experience to know what to do, the rest of the Vietnamese cowered belly down in the water behind the dike. I had already noted that they had neither machine guns to support an assault on us nor radios with which they might call in help. They were trapped. Nothing but open rice paddies lay all around them. They couldn't even stick up their heads to look around without getting zapped. The sun was going to get hot enough during the day to boil them.

I looked at Burke. He nodded. It was time to change positions. Staying under cover, we low-crawled to a new hide fifty meters to the left of the old and tunneled into the underbrush. The hamburgers hadn't stirred.

"Maybe they'll accept the bluff that there's a bunch of us strung out all along this ridge," I said. "Better keep an eye peeled on our flanks though. They could have friendlies around."

It turned into a waiting game. The sun climbed into a sky so hard the blue seemed to have been leached out of it. Even in the shade, Burke and I were sweating. I could only imagine how hot it must be out there in the rice fields. It had to be over one hundred degrees. The hamburgers had to be running low on water. If they ran out and tried to drink the fetid rice water, it would make them sick and dehydrate them all the more. The Vietnamese farmers used human shit and every other kind of crap for fertilizer.

Insects hummed. Steam rose from the rice paddies, inscribing transparent etchings between us and them. We kept an eye open on the surrounding wood lines for signs of enemy reinforcements, but nothing moved in the scattering of hootches in the tree line nearly two klicks away across the flats. Nothing moved in the rice field either. Hour after hour passed. I opened a can of peanut butter and ate it on crackers.

"They are scared shitless," Burke said wryly.

In the meantime, our sitreps radioed in to Hill 55 had set things to buzzing. Sparrowhawk was chomping at the bit. Their commander wanted to chopper-in on the trapped NVA, but I couldn't see getting Marines killed needlessly.

"Not yet," I advised. "I think we can hold them right here as long as we want them."

"You're calling the shots," came back the reply.

We were at that, weren't we?

It got hotter.

At midafternoon, somebody at the dike raised his head to test the waters. After I let him check it two or three more times without firing, he grew bold enough to rise cautiously to one knee with his head and chest above the dike. He looked around. He tugged his turtle helmet lower over his eyes against the sun and gave Dong Den a good scrutiny. I watched him through my rifle scope. I saw him chattering animatedly at the others, who still wouldn't stick up their heads. The corpses beginning to bloat among them were telling testimony against becoming too brave. I could almost imagine the bold one chiding his comrades:

"We're fools lying here in the water. There is nobody out there now. Let's go. We'll tell our commanders we were attacked by a battallion of Americans. Look, I'll prove it to you. I'm going to stand up right here and show you nothing will happen."

He slowly stood up and took a step up onto the dike. His khakis had turned dark from being water soaked.

I thought another one or two might follow him and Burke and I could cut down their numbers some more, but when no one else budged, I took aim on the brave one and squeezed the trigger gently. The bullet tore the hamburger's throat out of his collarbone in an explosion of red spray. He toppled out of sight behind the dike.

After that, I don't think you could have used dynamite to dislodge the others from cover. They were likely awaiting darkness to conceal their escape. We nipped that hope quickly by directing artillery to keep the skies above the valley blazing with 105-millimeter flares.

The flares were like brilliant miniature suns. As soon as some of them started settling, trailing smoke, sending black-and-white shadows swaying and dancing across the rice waters, fresh suns took their places. I doubt if the hamburgers got any sleep. Every hour or so either Burke or I, whichever of us was on watch, fired a round to let them know we were ready to send to his ancestors any other hot dog who even thought about showing himself.

The second day started the same as the first, except

the sun came out hotter than before. What started as sniping had become a siege. By ten o'clock, the mercury was reaching for the one hundred degree mark. We glimpsed some movement behind the dike, just flashes of it here and there. It was the first anything had occurred since I shot down the bold one yesterday afternoon.

"They're up to something," Burke said.

Just what soon became apparent. Eight khaki-clad recruits popped up from behind the dike on command and started a charge toward our tree line. They were yelling and screaming and firing their AKs, but the charge was kept in slow motion by the knee-deep water. Their turtles bounced on their heads. It was 700 meters from the dike to the forest, just short of a half mile. The fastest men in the world can run a half mile in less than two minutes—on hard surface under ideal conditions. It would have taken this bunch five minutes. They were further handicapped by the fact that they had chosen the wrong section of the tree line to attack. Burke and I watched them angling off from us at a forty-five degree angle. They were shooting up a patch of totally inoffensive jungle when we started our slaughter, methodically dropping six of them before they had covered 100 meters.

The two survivors turned and headed back to the dike; one of them made it. I felled the other one on top of the dike. His body lay there for the rest of the time, with his head and shoulders out of sight and his ass and legs protruding over the top. It bloated in the hot sun. The temperature must have reached 120 degrees out there. Clouds of black flies swarmed above the corpses. The bodies would be filled with maggots by another morning.

"Them hamburgers are *suffering*," Burke commented, not without sympathy.

Burke and I changed sites again, working our way around the broadly curving base of Dong Den in hopes of exposing the NVA's left flank to our fire. You never stay in the same hide after you've fired from there. It took us more than two hours to complete the move of three hundred yards. The new hide offered only a slight advantage over the old in terms of a better field of fire. The dike still protected the recruits; flies buzzed above the dozen or so corpses we had contributed to fertilizing the rice fields.

One of us dozed through the steamy afternoon while the other kept watch.

Fog began creeping into the valley as darkness fell on the second night of the siege. It muted the bright white light of the flares hanging in the sky from dusk to dawn. We kept expecting the remaining NVA to make a run for it. They were not likely to get a better chance.

Not one of them took it.

On the third morning, five of the soldiers tried charging the tree line again. As before, they attacked the wrong place. Apparently, two days of heat, thirst, and carnage had driven them mad. They were stumbling as they splashed in slow motion through the rice water. We killed them so casually I was almost ashamed of it.

Nature promised some relief in the afternoon when distant thunder rumbled down the Cade and clouds bunched into anvils around the rim of the bowl made by the surrounding mountains. For over seven hours, since the suicidal charge of that morning, the enemy had not stirred. They lay unshaded and baking in the midday heat, each hour making their situation all the more hopeless, teased by the promise of rain, taunted by the flow of the river just a short walk away.

Burke wiped sweat and squinted at the distant rain

clouds. The air was oppressive and supercharged, the way it is before a storm.

"A little rain would feel good," Burke said.

I nodded grimly. "Think what it'd do for them hamburgers out there."

Burke studied the clouds some more. "Reckon they'll try to make a run for it if the storm blows in?"

"Wouldn't you, if that's the only chance you had?"

All we could do was wait. The waiting must have been torture for the hamburgers. Soon, the distant clouds kicked up a feisty breeze. It was as hot as the breath of a furnace, not cool like it should have been coming out of rain. We were downwind. The breeze wafted across the paddies and brought the stench of the rice fields to our nostrils. It testified more than any words to the hell the NVA soldiers were enduring. We smelled the rotting of the corpses and of men who, though still alive, were rotting a little anyhow from stewing in the stagnant water for the past three days. Necessity forced them to relieve themselves in their pants. Some were undoubtedly sick and vomiting from drinking the poison water.

The stink was overpowering. Burke retched and clasped his hand over his mouth and nose. Later, we learned that patrols from as far as five miles away were able to smell Elephant Valley all that week.

The rainstorm rumbled and played around in the mountains. A few raindrops skittered across the rice water, teasing, and then the clouds coasted down the far side of the mountains and the sun returned hotter than ever.

"Poor bastards," Burke mumbled.

That night, we used a new tactic. Instead of keeping the valley lit up with flares, we let periods of darkness lure the NVA into attempting escape. Twice we let them glimpse freedom, only to jerk it away from them

149

at the last moment. The hamburgers looked like deer paralyzed by headlights when flares exploded into suns, catching them in the open. Shooting them was as easy as jacklighting deer. We dropped the leaders until the survivors milled and turned back to the dike.

On their third escape attempt, the recruits used one squad as a diversion. Flares caught them in the open, but the rest of the NVA were waiting behind the dike ready to open up on our muzzle flashes. For the first time since the siege began, we had bullets cutting through the trees and brush all around us.

"Get the hell out?" Burke called.

"Not yet. Keep dinging 'em."

If they charged this time, supported by increasingly accurate cover fire, we had no choice but to pull back, and in a hurry, to save our own skins. But until that happened, we popped off the hamburgers caught in the open until those who were left once more scurried back to the dike.

The flares sizzled into darkness. Firing from the dike ceased. Burke and I lay quietly listening for any sounds of an attack, ready to slip out the back door and call in an artillery barrage on the valley. Gradually, however, after listening to croaking gecko lizards and tree frogs for some time, we began to relax, concluding that the NVA, or at least what remained of them, had had enough for one night.

The siege continued.

By this time, almost every U.S. Marine unit in Vietnam must have known about Elephant Valley and the NVA company trapped there. They were radioing sitreps to each other about it while they waited expectantly for an outcome that even Burke and I could not predict at the present. Either the survivors were hard pressed and desperate enough to try literally *anything* within the next few hours in order to escape, or they were so demoralized that from now on killing them would be like slaughtering penned cattle.

I sympathized with them. I looked at Burke and knew how I must also appear to him. He was gaunt from the strain of the last few days, his eyes dark circles in his face. We were running low on food and water and ammunition. Although we rotated rest cycles—one watching and one napping—what rest we managed had been fitful and sporadic. As bad off as we were, the NVA had to be tenfold worse.

We decided to continue the siege for at least one more day. Sparrowhawk was eager to come to our relief.

We changed positions again during the night since the hamburgers knew where we were. After daylight came, we picked off two or three more enemy soldiers who foolishly exposed themselves to fire at our old hide. Then quiet and the heat settled over the fourth day. The corpses out in the rice fields were bloated to the size of water buffalos. Occasionally, a stray breeze gagged us with the smell.

Early in the afternoon while I was on watch, I glimpsed about an inch of a man's head as he tried to get a look around. I took aim.

"I'm going to drop him if he pokes up again."

Burke looked skeptical. A shot like that was like shooting a postcard a half mile away.

Presently, the head eased into view again. I squeezed the trigger. Burke stared wordlessly when the head exploded in a cloud of brains, bone, and blood.

Then he said, "You got him!" Like he still didn't believe it.

I wasn't sure I believed it either, but I didn't let on.

"Fascinating, isn't it?" I said, grinning.

Later in the day, no doubt driven by thirst and

despair, about ten of the young Vietnamese soldiers leaped to their feet on cue and fled toward the river. A couple of them didn't even bother to bring their weapons. All ten died. The odds were getting more and more in our favor.

About 8:20 P.M., just as illumination rounds were lighting up Elephant Valley for the fourth night in a row, the NVA opened up with a hail of fire that chewed savagely at the deadwood behind which Burke and I lay concealed.

"They've pinpointed us. Let's *move!*"

Burke covered while I slithered through the undergrowth to a new hide fifty feet away. Then I covered for him until he joined me. We had just set up again behind a felled tree when the NVA attacked across the long expanse of paddies beneath the white hot light from the flares. There weren't many of them left, I saw, and what there was of them had turned suicidal. I sat cross-legged and used the fallen tree as a bench rest while Burke crawled into a sinkhole surrounded by roots and brush and covered with vines. He used the mound in front of him as a rest for his M-14.

My first shot sent the lead soldier tumbling head over heels, like a rabbit shot on the run. He lay screaming and splashing in the water as he died. A second soldier dropped onto his knees next to his wounded friend. My next bullet caught this one in the chest. He reeled over backwards with his legs folded underneath.

A few of the soldiers made it back to the dike.

The slow drizzle that began falling after midnight must have been a welcome relief for the ten or twelve sick and exhausted NVA who had so far managed to survive. It was much less so for Burke and me. I lay in the mud with the light steady rain soaking to my bones and I started to shiver. Burke turned a sunken, unshaved face toward me. The fatigue hollows in it became all the more dramatic in the eerie, shifting light of the ever-present flares.

"We've had enough," I said.

As soon as light broke on the fifth morning, Burke radioed the artillery battery to give us a few minutes and then rain HE into the rice paddies. With one last look across the gridded water-covered flats dotted by the bloated bodies of the many enemy soldiers we had killed, we turned and silently stepped into the jungle. It would be hours before the few remaining recruits knew we were gone. By then, it would be too late for them.

Burke and I picked our way around the base of Dong Den to rendezvous with a jubilant patrol that would escort us back to Hill 55. We paused once to listen to the rumbling thunder of the cannon shells exploding on the dike.

"Them poor bastards."

Apparently, the only survivor of their five days of hell was one supply sergeant whom Sparrowhawk found hiding among the farmers' hootches by the river. Trembling from fright and weakness, he refused to believe that his company had been wiped out by *two* men with rifles.

"I know only if somebody showed himself, even a bit, he died," lamented the lone NVA survivor of the Elephant Valley massacre.

CHAPTER SIXTEEN

U.S. Marine Lance Corporal
Jim Miller
Vietnam, 1968

The CH-46 choppered down and slicked into a clearing, depending upon your definition of *clearing*. I immediately understood why elephant grass was called elephant grass; you could *hide* an elephant in it. I cringed when the helicopter settled and the back ramp dropped. In-country only three weeks, I half expected little yellow men to run out and start shooting at me while I fired one accurate shot at a time, like they taught in sniper school.

Nothing happened though, except the helicopter blades flattened the tall grass in a big circle around the bird. I squared my shoulders and prepared to trot down the ramp with my Remington 700 in a case to protect it. *Murder Incorporated,* they sometimes called us because we carried our rifles in cases.

A line company of the Seventh Marine Regiment needed snipers, requested them—and I was one they were receiving. Short, blond, baby-faced Miller who didn't have to shave but maybe once a month.

"I don't care if you are a sniper and I don't care if that's nothing but peach fuzz on your face—go shave!" the platoon sergeant growled when I reported in on Hill 55. His name was Puckett. He later became Sergeant Major of the Marine Corps.

I wanted to make a good impression on my first sniper mission. I was looking pretty good, like I wasn't even afraid, when I came charging down that helicopter ramp and gave a little hop at the end of the ramp into the flattened grass, hanging onto my rifle with one hand and my helmet with the other to keep the blade turbulence from kicking off my headgear and demolishing what dignity I possessed. Other combat grunts were watching me offload.

I gave that last little jaunty hop into the grass—and promptly disappeared into a bomb crater left from some previous B-52 strike. I heard somebody snicker as the chopper clawed back into the sky and I came crawling out of the crater on my hands and knees.

"Miller, huh? We're gonna be here awhile, lad. Go dig in."

Dig in? Snipers didn't dig in. Digging in implied hand-to-hand combat, grenades, machine guns, and all that. Snipers did their duty from 'way back. We believed long distance was the next best thing to being there.

I dug in. At least I *started* to dig in. The company was supposed to be holding this hill or something. The grunts had fighting holes dug all around its crest. One look told me this wasn't a good place for a sniper to be. Hills rode each other right up into the face of the hill we were on, like a bunch of Barnum and Bailey circus elephants mounted on top of each other. They were all ragged and matted with jungle. Digging in meant you expected the little yellow men to get *close* to you.

My E-tool struck something. I prodded around in the damp earth for a little while, then dug some more. I hadn't gone very deep. I tossed out a shovelful of dirt from around whatever it was that occupied this hole before I got to it, then bent over for another. I scraped the dirt away from whatever it was I was uncovering.

"*Good God!*"

A human skull was looking up at me with this big wide *gotcha!* grin. The whole skeleton was there.

I *evacuated* that hole.

I spent the night on *flat* ground. I had had my fill of holes.

The company didn't need snipers after all. They needed bulldozers and jungle men. After a few days lying around, I choppered out and over to 3/7 near Hill 112 and Antenna Valley. It was open ground with squares of rice paddies, many well-used trails, and no reported friendlies in the area other than us. That meant anyone you saw who didn't look like you was presumed to be the enemy. You couldn't even be sure of the villagers.

I didn't have to dig any holes. The company I was with in 3/7 pushed farther south toward the Phu Son complex. *Pushed* meant you walked. Another sniper and I tagged along because there wasn't anything else we could do.

The company spread out on line and began sweeping toward Phu Son 6. A village complex often had several hamlets all with the same name, so we numbered them. Five VC flushed from a line of bamboo that ran around the ville. They were dressed in black pajamas and carried AKs. They were only about two hundred meters out in front of us.

I figured it was about time to show the company what Murder Incorporated could do. I stepped forward out of the line and with complete self-assurance swung my Remington 700 to my shoulder. I captured one of the running VC in the scope's clear, round sight picture.

I eased in pressure on the trigger.

Before I could fire, the world *exploded* around me.

"Good God!"

The pain is excruciating when you think your brain is squirting out through ruptured ear drums. It blinds you. I dropped my rifle and grabbed my ears with both hands as I fell to my knees. I knelt there in the grass trying to sort out what happened.

It seemed my partner had opened up with *his* 700 against the VC the instant before I was going to fire. That took care of my right ear. The machine gunner took care of the other ear with his M-60. It was a conspiracy against my ear drums.

They didn't get the VC either.

"This sniper shit has got to get better," my partner said, disappointed.

"What?" I said. "What did you say?"

I had been in Vietnam three months without firing one shot in anger, as they say, when I found myself and my 700 standing tower watch—*tower watch*—back on Hill 55. It was a hot day when the air kind of hummed and sizzled in your ears. I was restless. I paced the three or four steps back and forth inside the little cupola on stilts that lets you look out over the wire and mines and see the dinks that might be trying to sneak up through the elephant grass. You zap them before they get close enough to zap you. It was kind of a weird game.

Through my big ship binoculars—the kind used on the bridge of warships—I could see every blade of knife grass growing on the undulating flats in front of me. I don't know how the three gooks out there thought they could escape detection. One of them wore a *white* shirt. I counted the buttons on it where it bulged out over an M-79 grenade launcher he was trying to conceal underneath it. The wooden stock stuck out in front below his shirt.

It was obvious what the gooks were doing. They were trying to get close enough to rocket the Marine emplacements behind me. They darted and scurried through the grass like field mice in a hay meadow avoiding an owl.

I was the owl.

The range was about 1,250 meters. It was a long shot, but I thought I could make it. I peered at the VC through my rifle scope. It was a nine power, zeroed in at 1,000 meters. That meant if I wanted to shoot a gook at a range of 500 meters, I had to aim at his balls in order to get him in the chest. If I wanted to shoot one at 1,200 meters, I aimed at his head to get his heart. Simple arithmetic. It was balls below 1,000, head beyond 1,000, and heart *at* 1,000.

I sighted in on the dink wearing the white shirt/M-79 ensemble.

I fired one shot just as he turned his back to me to look toward his comrades. The bullet struck him in the back. He stumbled like a big fist had pounded him hard between his shoulder blades. He kept running; I jacked in a fresh full-metal jacket and fired again.

He dropped this time. You can only take getting pounded in the back so many times. The other two gooks, they *vanished*. I only *thought* I could see every blade of grass.

A squad went out to pick up the kill for a body count. I watched through binoculars from my cupola as the Marines searched in the tall grass. They got on line and searched. They tramped around in circles. Finally, they returned empty handed.

"Where *is* he?" I asked.

"You just thought you got him, deadeye."

"I didn't miss."

"Then where is he?"

Somebody told me the VC went to extraordinary efforts to recover their dead and wounded. They knew it was demoralizing to the Americans to shoot and shoot and never find any bodies.

"I *knew* I didn't miss," I gloated.

Action started picking up after that. In Bravo 1/7, Corporal Jay Taylor and I went hunting as part of a five-man killer team. There were two grunts, a radio man, and two snipers—Taylor and me. We patrolled out into Indian Country and set up on trails and other likely areas and waited on the stand until game came along and we got a shot. In the Phu Son area, you didn't have to worry about game conservation either. There was plenty of VC. You expected contact every time you went through the wire.

One hot afternoon—it was *always* hot in Vietnam, just some days were hotter than others—the killer team angled through a patch of jungle clotting the bottom of a draw and climbed at an angle the opposite rise. We had just left a particularly disappointing stand and were on our way home. The grunt on point reached the top of the knoll first and suddenly froze as he got a look across to the other side. He eased down to one knee and passed back the hand signal for *enemy near.*

The rest of us low-crawled to the knoll crest one at a time and parted the grass to take a look. We stared.

Just below us, a dozen VC, an entire squad, naked as the day they were whelped, were cavorting and having a good time in the brown shallow water of a jungle river. Their clothing and weapons lay in piles on the river bank.

"They're just asking for it," Taylor whispered.

I nodded slowly. "Then we wouldn't want to disappoint 'em."

The five of us got ready. We took aim. Rapid, accurate bursts of rifle fire shattered the VC's fun like a bomb in nursery school. The brown water boiled with the fury of the attack. The first ones hit churned the river as they died. They turned the water scarlet. Two or three actually made it to the bank, and, ignoring their clothing and weapons, ran for the cover of the jungle before we dropped them. We quickly finished off the wounded with a few sporadic shots, then decided if there was a squad here there might also be a platoon or a company.

We hightailed it off the knoll in a file down through the grass and through the jungle at the bottom of the draw. We were panting as we zigzagged up the opposite rise when the air split above us, like some giant was hurling refrigerators or Volkswagens at us. The decision to vacate the knoll had been a timely one. The entire top of it erupted like a big squeezed pimple or boil as enemy mortars demolished it.

I paused to look back at the smoke-and-dust cloud. If we had delayed there just *two* more minutes . . .

"Good God!"

I reported twelve kills to Hill 55. "They were in the river," I said. "They were all *clean* kills."

The commander of one of the companies I worked with was a by-the-book officer. He was so proud of being a captain that he even wore his bars in the field. I guess he wanted the VC to know it too. His men said he was a career asshole getting his ticket punched with combat time to help his promotions. That was all he cared about. Those kind will get you killed. I'm surprised somebody didn't frag him; somebody might have, later.

The company had been in the field about three days on a search-and-destroy mission. Most of it was just search. We worked our way by platoons off the top of a big hill and into a valley where a ville cozied up next to a narrow river. The hamlet appeared deserted. Abandoned villages were eerie. You never knew what would happen.

Weapons at the ready, eyes darting suspiciously, we entered the hamlet and swept slowly through the outskirts of grass-thatched or tin-roofed hootches. It was like the VC knew when we were coming and took everything with them, leaving behind not even a bare-assed chicken or one of those razorback-looking pigs. They cleared out. We passed through. They moved back in behind us. The only sounds anywhere in the village were muffled footfalls and the occasional clank of an M-16.

One of the guys came out of a hootch carrying some Cambodian school textbooks.

"We *are* still in Vietnam?" he asked.

"Who the fuck knows? If you've seen one Asian shithole, you've seen 'em all."

It was always a relief to leave one of those villages where you expected everything to be booby-trapped and get back into the bush. It started to get dark as the platoon weaved out the other side of the hamlet and twined its way up a hill. It gets dark fast in the bush. I found myself hoping we'd come to the top of the hill and find an old firebase with the fighting holes already dug. I had developed an aversion to digging holes after my experience with the skeleton. That would be happiness—a double-decker hole already dug to hide in for the night and a C-rat can of beanie-wienies. That was about as safe and comfortable as you could get in the bush.

Still, I remembered the last time we found an abandoned firebase. One of the guys dozed off and was awakened by somebody rummaging through his pack, stealing beanie-wienies or something. Furious, he jumped up with the intent of giving the thief a sound whacking. The CO had to medevac the Marine for treatment of combat injuries. You don't *ever* want to lay hands on a four-foot-tall, ninety-pound *rock ape* and expect to give *him* any kind of whacking.

It just went to prove that in the bush nowhere was safe.

The company came to the top of the hill by platoons. The dying sun shone red on a bare hilltop pockmarked with craters from a past bombing. The chickenshit captain had us move into a perimeter. We didn't dig in though. We just collapsed into old bomb craters and dropped exhausted behind the nearest bush. I found a fallen tree to share with my partner Taylor. I loosed my pack and fell on top of it behind the mossy tree trunk. I took a deep breath, scratched where the pack straps had rubbed me raw, and casually glanced over the terrain.

"Good God!"

A narrow, deep gorge dropped off in front of me. Messing around in the bush on the steep opposite rise were five NVA soldiers dressed in khaki uniforms. They were only about two hundred meters away across the ravine. They were so preoccupied with whatever they were doing that they hadn't seen or heard an entire *company* of Marines setting up right under their yellow noses.

I was almost afraid to move.

"Gooks!" I whispered to my partner as I eased my 700 across the top of the tree trunk.

The 9X scope brought them right into my face. Two were officers decked out in bright red lapels and stars. I settled my cross hairs on the one wearing a pistol with a red star on the grips. At that range, I dropped the cross hairs to his nuts.

I fired.

He went down hard with his chest blown open.

My second shot picked off the second officer.

The surviving gooks recovered from their surprise enough to chatter at us a moment with their AKs, but then they disappeared. My first shot attracted the asshole captain, who had been puttering around nearby. He whirled in time to see me down the second officer. He fired a few rounds in the gooks' direction, then dashed over and skidded down behind the tree trunk next to me.

"I got one! I got one!" he shouted. "Did you see it? I got an officer!"

What the fuck was he talking about?

"Captain, they're *both* mine," I said.

"No! I got one. I want that SKS rifle."

"How could you tell it was an SKS? You couldn't even see it."

"*Corporal*, I want that SKS. *I* got one confirmed kill, *you* got *one*. Do I make myself clear?"

I guess it would look good in his file. What he was saying was that I either settled for one confirmed kill or *neither* of us got one. I had to make the deal. Besides, what difference did it make?

"Yes, *sir*," I said.

In the meantime, every grunt on my side of the hill was working off his frustrations by getting in a little trigger time. That was SOP, standard operating procedure. When things settled down, the captain was grinning and satisfied with the deal he made with me. He jumped up and ran off to saddle up a squad to go

check the bodies and recover the SKS he thought he
had. Taylor and I didn't wait. We scouted down into
the gorge and climbed up to where I had made the
kills. The captain's squad followed about a hundred
meters behind. It was rugged terrain, and we had to
hurry before it got dark.

Pools of bright blood on the vegetation marked the
correct location, but the bodies were gone. We followed the blood trail to a spider trap that turned out to
be the entrance to a tunnel complex. The entire hill
must have been hollow. Grenades dropped down the
hole exploded so deep underground that we could
hardly hear the muffled reports.

A tunnel rat I wasn't.

"I ain't going down there either," Taylor said.

The captain came huffing up the hill with his squad.
His head swiveled back and forth on his shoulders as
he searched frantically for the gook corpses.

"Where are they?" he demanded. "Where's the
rifle?"

I looked at him. I grinned as I pointed at the entrance to the tunnel.

"It's down there if you want to go in and get it."

I guess he thought long distance was the next best
thing to being there too.

CHAPTER SEVENTEEN

On his way to take command of the First Marine Division at Chu Lai, Vietnam, in 1966, Major General Herman Nickerson, Jr. stopped off at Okinawa where Captain Jim Land commanded the Third Force Service Regiment Ordnance Company. The general quietly surveyed the muscular man who had worked his way up through the ranks from private to an officer's commission. He liked what he saw—the flattop bristling off into gray stubble at the temples, the determination in the English bulldog face.

Whether you were officer or enlisted, here stood a man upon whom you could depend.

"Captain Land, I have an assignment for you. I want you to organize a sniper unit within the First Division. Captain Bob Russell in the Third Division started training snipers last year. I want *mine* to be the best in the Marine Corps. I want them killing VC and I don't care how they do it—even if you have to go out and do it yourself."

Jim Land had been studying and teaching the nearly

lost art and science of the sniper's trade since 1959. A marksman himself, he held Distinguished Division medals and had been captain of the Pacific Division shooting team. He and Sergeant Carlos Hathcock shot together for the Marine Corps team at the National Matches at Camp Perry. Hathcock went on to win the 1965 Wimbledon Cup for the best long-range rifle shot and the one thousand yard Championship while Land was captain of the Marine Corps pistol team.

Land founded and commanded the scout/sniper school in Hawaii in 1960, the only such school in the Army or Marine Corps at the time. Its second class graduated Carlos Hathcock. As soon as the Vietnam War began, Land started looking for a way to launch snipers into combat. It was his experience and research that provided Captain Bob Russell's Third Division sniper school with many of its materials, including lessons from his Hawaii school, copies of *The British Sniper Manual*, and other World War II era publications. Land had read and studied everything he could find on the subject. He particularly depended upon the World War I experiences of Captain Herbert W. McBride.

Now, General Nickerson was giving him the opportunity to put his training and theories into practice with his own sniper school.

Captain Land arrived in Vietnam in September 1966 and started from scratch through trial and error in building a school that became the prototype for the first permanent sniper school in the history of the American armed forces. Since there was no table of equipment officially authorized for the fledgling school, Land had to cajole and finagle equipment and weapons from reluctant and misunderstanding superiors whose war aims were directed elsewhere. He finally managed to acquire a supply of Winchester

30.06 Model 70 hunting rifles that the division kept in special services for its troops to check out for deer hunting. Then he discovered there were no ordnance funds available with which to purchase telescopic sights. He used recreation funds for that, sending men to the post exchange in Okinawa to buy scopes along with volleyball nets and basketballs.

"Sniping as recreation," he grumbled.

He was selecting an instructor staff at the same time he was accumulating equipment and having firing ranges built and classroom GPs set up on Hill 55. He knew what he wanted in his instructors. He wanted mature combat riflemen who had previously been competitive marksmen, men who knew the fundamentals of sharpshooting and could *do* what they were expected to teach. One of the first shooter/instructors he chose was 24-year-old Carlos Hathcock, who at the time was a dissatisfied MP in Chu Lai. Other known Marine shooting experts like Master Sergeant Donald L. Reinke and Staff Sergeant Charles A. Roberts soon completed his seventeen-member staff.

He still was not ready to open his school to accept students. Although his staff had expertise in shooting and were combat Marines, the only one among them who had done any sniping at all was Hathcock. Hathcock had already picked off a number of enemy soldiers around Chu Lai while working as an MP. Even Land, who had been teaching sniping and shooting for at least the past seven years, had no practical experience in the hunting and shooting of other armed men.

That was something he intended to correct. His men, before they *taught* snipers, would first *become* snipers. He paired the men and sent them into the bush to personally learn the trade. Land went with them.

"Reinke," he said. "Let's go hunting."

On their first experience-gaining hunt, the two men selected a good hide in the bush that afforded natural camouflage and adequate fields of fire. After a wait of about two hours, Land picked up movement through his spotting scope. Reinke was going to do the first shooting.

"There's one," the captain whispered.

Reinke scanned the distance through his rifle scope. "Where?"

"To your left front," Land clarified.

"I don't see him," Reinke replied through clenched teeth.

"Goddamnit, he's standing right there by that fucking tree."

"There's a whole goddamned fucking forest out there, Cap'n."

Land attempted to direct Reinke to the VC's location and Reinke tried to find it. The two men grew more frustrated with each passing second. By the time Reinke located the *right* tree, the VC had vanished into the forest.

In their haste to gain experience and get the program started, they had neglected one of the sniper's most important tasks—laying out a range card with zones and reference points that would have enabled the spotter to instantly put the shooter on target with just a few words: "Zone two, point three, forty meters left."

But that was how they and the other sniper instructors personally learned the lessons they would be passing on to their sniper students about shooting and marksmanship and the psychology and lore of hunting the most dangerous big game of all. They took to the jungles and fields of Vietnam and, gaining experience as they went, soon made themselves experts in the sniper's deadly art. During that early three-month period, Land's seventeen-man instructor cadre killed more VC than any battalion in I Corps. The snipers would work a particular area for three to five days and then move on to another sector. When they returned to the original sector as long as two months later, they found the local VC and NVA still sneaking around and ducking at every sudden noise.

Little of what the instructors were learning was especially new. Baron Steinfurst-Wallenstein had learned it in 1870, McBride in World War I, John Fulcher in World War II, and Chet Hamilton in Korea. However, in relearning the art and science, the snipers converted their knowledge to lessons to be taught and thus made a commitment to keeping it alive.

McBride, for example, had discovered that firing across an obstacle such as a tree, boulder, ditch, or creek made the shot seem to originate from there instead of from its true location. Land's snipers relearned that valuable lesson when one of them fired past a forest monarch at a band of VC and missed. The VC returned fire at the tree, riddling it and the surrounding forest, but did not send a single shot in the direction of the sniper's actual hide.

That valuable lesson would be passed on to students.

Previous marksmen as far back as the American Revolutionary War had studied the trajectory of bullets and how wind, humidity, and temperature affected trajectory. Weather conditions became even more critical on the flight of a bullet as modern technology increased the range a bullet could be hurled. Land and his instructors drafted lesson plans based on shooting at various wind velocities and temperatures. If the wind was blowing toward the sniper, they learned, the bullet had a tendency to rise. If the wind was blowing from behind, the bullet dropped. Temperature as much as wind became critical at ranges beyond six hundred yards. The bullet rode differently on a warm, bright morning than it did on a cool, overcast evening.

Ammunition itself made a difference in accuracy, especially at long ranges. Land ordered match-grade boat-tailed ammo in lots. Match-grade ammo was carefully manufactured to permit predictable results from one cartridge to the next.

Land discovered new, more effective ways of sighting-in rifles and scopes: "You sight your rifle in at 450 yards and then use a center hold for 100 yards to 450 yards. The only time you need readjust your sights is for shots longer than 600 yards."

He experimented with telescopic sights and made recommendations that were to be incorporated much later in the Marine Corps sniper's "dream rifle." Since a shooter tended to lose the fine cross hairs in failing light, Land suggested sniper scopes be equipped with inverted posts instead of cross hairs. The inverted post allowed the shooter to "hold over" his target at long ranges without blocking sight of the target.

There was one particular area of the snipers' trade which Land and his sniper instructors explored that had rarely been touched on previously. It was something, Land felt, that was just as important as how to zero a weapon or how a bullet flew through the air. It was the psychological makeup of the prospective sniper. What, Land asked himself, did it take emotionally and mentally for a man to coolly take aim and calculatedly blast another man out of this world and into another? What kind of man did it take to be a sniper and not be destroyed by it?

"It takes a special kind of courage to be alone—to be alone with your fears, to be alone with your doubts," Jim Land wrote. "There is no one from whom you can draw strength except yourself. This courage is not the often seen, superficial brand, stimulated by the flow of adrenaline. And neither is it the courage that comes from the fear that others might think you a coward.

"For the sniper, there is no hate of the enemy, only respect of him or her as a quarry. Psychologically, the only motive that will sustain the sniper is knowing he is doing a necessary job and having the confidence that he is the best person to do it. On the battlefield, hate will destroy any man—especially a sniper. Killing for revenge will ultimately twist his mind.

"The sniper is the big game hunter of the battlefield. He uses all of those skills regularly studied, admired, and accepted by people who would apply them to hunting deer, elk, or perhaps bear. Certainly, the sniper, like the big game hunter, must know and understand the habits of the quarry which he hunts. He must possess the field craft to be able to successfully position himself for a killing shot. Finally, the sniper must have highly developed marksmanship skills to effectively place a single bullet into his intended target. In short, a sniper must be self-reliant and possess the keen skills of a still hunter or poacher."

Major R. O. "Dick" Culver, who, after the war, joined with Land to establish the U.S. Marine Corps Scout/Sniper School at Quantico and put together what is today the most powerful, most accurate sniper rifle in the world, added his own observations to Land's.

"As far as the psychological aspect," he said, "the sniper must feel that he can kill when the time comes. He has to have no compunction against killing, but must also have compassion. He has to have a conscience, not necessarily a tremendously religious person, but one who kills wantonly is worthless. You don't want a man who will kill for the sake of killing.''

"When you look through that scope," Land concluded, "the first thing you see is the eyes. There is a lot of difference between shooting at a shadow, shooting at an outline, and shooting at a pair of eyes. It is amazing when you put that scope on somebody, the first thing that pops out at you is the eyes. Many men can't do it at that point.''

In all previous wars, and even within selected units in Vietnam, snipers were more or less selected at random, the only qualification seeming to be that of a high score on the boot camp rifle range. When Captain Land began accepting sniper students for his school on Hill 55, he chose candidates who were already reasonably good with a rifle but who were not necessarily experts. "You can always teach him to shoot better if he has proper hand-eye coordination." What Land was looking for in his candidates went deeper than mere shooting, as he explained to Hathcock, Reinke, and the other instructors:

"I want each man screened when he comes in. When they arrive, I'll interview them, then you take them over to the 'club' and shoot the shit. You can find out more than I can in the formal interview. I want them to be stable, intelligent, and, above all, know their way around in the field. Mentally, I don't want anyone who signs up because he has a score to settle. I want men who come to us because there is a job to do.''

In addition, Land wanted the candidates to be right-handed, primarily because most rifles are made for right-handed shooters, with the bolt handle on the right side. His candidates should not wear glasses. Glasses could be lost, broken, fogged at a critical moment, or catch the glint of the sun to betray a sniper's position. Snipers should not be heavy tobacco users. Smokers became nervous and fidgety whenever they were unable to light up, such as during a long wait in a hide. Cigarette smoke could also betray a sniper by its odor or its telltale trail escaping from an otherwise camouflaged location. And most of all, the prospective sniper must have patience of the kind that John Unertl demonstrated when he sat for three days in a hide and crapped in his pants rather than risk exposing himself before he got his shot.

"You can't let anything else enter your mind except your job," Carlos Hathcock said. "You even have to turn off your sex drive."

Each of the sniper courses on Hill 55 lasted two weeks, during which time students learned their skills and were then "tested" by venturing into the bush with an instructor to kill VC from hiding. From September 1966 to April 1967, Land and his cadre trained over six hundred snipers, including Marines, Army GIs, ARVN, and other allies. Snipers in Vietnam began taking a toll from the enemy far out of proportion to their actual numbers.

"Most of the snipers developed a much higher level of concentration and discipline than the average infantryman," said Land. "The thing that set Carlos Hathcock off from the others was his extremely high level of concentration and total awareness of his surroundings. He had a remarkable singleness of purpose."

Land tried to instill and maintain that singleness of purpose in all his snipers. He would not let them go on R and R (Rest and Recuperation) because he felt it would be dangerous for them to leave the field and lose that keen survival edge that kept them alive in the bush. The only thing he wanted them thinking about was killing the enemy. He didn't want them in a hide mooning over some girl in a bar in Okinawa. The closest thing he had to a mutiny was when Bob Hope brought his USO show to Vietnam and he refused to let his snipers attend.

In spite of Captain Land's rigorous selection process and his precautions in choosing sniper candidates, he was bound to have some failures. One of them was a corporal named "Robert M." who came to sniper school and then stayed in the sniper platoon. Over a period of a few weeks, he proved himself by accumulating a kill count of seven VC.

Marines were having some problems with VC in a valley not far from Hill 55. The enemy roamed freely among the villages and rice paddies, disappearing into the surrounding hills whenever Marine forces swept through it. As soon as the Marines left, however, the VC immediately reappeared.

"Why don't we set up some snipers in the hills as a blocking force?" Land suggested. "Old Nguyen Schwartz knows where the grunts are all the time, but he may not be able to detect our sniper teams."

Several two-man teams used the cover of darkness to slip into the forest that covered the hills opposite where the Marines would begin their sweep. As expected, the Viet Cong evacuated the valley ahead of the advancing Marines, driven directly into the sights of the accurate rifles hidden in the bush. Corporal Robert M. killed eleven enemy soldiers during the course of that bloody day.

A couple of days later, Captain Land called an equipment inspection. His men were about to disperse into the field on another mission. One of the snipers missed formation. Land sent a man to find Corporal Robert M. The man returned alone. He looked stunned.

"Skipper, you'd better come take a look."

Hathcock was the school's NCOIC. "Carlos, go see

what's going on," Land said, continuing his inspection.

Hathcock strode into Robert M.'s tent and stopped with his hand still on the tent flap. Robert M. huddled on the ground at the far end of the tent. He had his poncho pulled over his head.

"Bob?"

The figure did not stir. Hathcock walked over and gently shook him. Still no response. Corporal Robert M., who had been such an outstanding sniper student and who had done so well with eleven kills at the valley "turkey shoot," had gone catatonic.

The division psychologist back at Chu Lai later explained to Captain Land what happened.

"Corporal M. never told you, but after he had only been in-country for a little while, one of his buddies stepped on a mine that killed him and his lieutenant. He couldn't do a thing about it since all the line troops see most of the time are shadows, moving bushes, and muzzle flashes. Corporal M. wanted to see his enemy die. He joined the snipers to get even."

Robert M. got even with seventeen personal kills. He got even for his buddy. He got even for his lieutenant. He got even for himself. He kept getting even until his mind simply snapped from the bloodletting.

After awhile, the corporal seemed to have recovered. He was at Chu Lai about to be released to return to his original outfit—not the snipers—when two Reuters correspondents came to interview him for a feature article. Robert M. got through the interview up to the point where one of the journalists cleared his throat and abruptly asked:

"What is it like to take another human being's life?"

The Marine's body instantly stiffened. His eyes darted wildly about the room, as though looking for a place to hide. Finding nothing, he retreated inwardly.

He suddenly relaxed. His eyes turned dull and still, as though whatever life force existed to animate them had drained away in the space of one heartbeat.

Corporal Robert M., ex-sniper who knew seventeen times what it was like to kill with one accurate sniper's shot at a time, did not want to remember ever again those eyes he had seen through his rifle scope.

"Corporal? Corporal?"

There was no response.

CHAPTER EIGHTEEN

U.S. Marine Captain
Jim Land
Vietnam, 1966

Hill 55 rose out of the green Vietnamese countryside just north of where the Yen and La Tho Rivers junctioned at a fat Y. The hill resembled a huge hand severed from its arm at the wrist. Its coarse fingers clutched at the fertile rice fields and clumps of jungle and bamboo in the lowlands that surrounded it. The Marines who occupied the hilltop against both jungle and VC had numbered each of the fingers. Finger One reached southeast almost to the La Tho River. Finger Two was a short, skinny thumb. Finger Three stretched northeast toward the village complexes of Thai Cam and Bich Bac.

Before the sniper school opened on the hill, the VC were free to use their own snipers against the entrenched Marines. Finger One in particular had suffered, since the VC could use jungle and river growth to approach within easy rifle range. The first request Marine commanders made of us when I started assembling a sniper cadre was that we take care of the enemy sniper who plagued Finger One. Just within the past two weeks he had killed two Marines and wounded two others. The grunts had been unable to locate his hide and eliminate him. Marines on the finger darted about like mice afraid to show themslyes to a cat whose taloned paws were capable of swatting them at will.

Sergeant Don Reinke and I shouldered our equipment and made our way cautiously out to the line of bunkers and fighting holes that jointed the finger and almost severed it in places.

"We got a problem," one of the platoon leaders said in greeting. "We had a gunnery sergeant shot while loading a truck, a captain took a round leaving the crapper, a squad leader was killed here on the finger, and two troops have been wounded."

"That makes *five*," I pointed out.

"Yes, sir. We had one more hit since we called for you guys. Just don't walk around up here anywhere in the open. He'll damned sure get you."

First on a map while we hid in a sandbagged bunker and then from a protected vantage point on the hill, the platoon leader showed us the lay of the land around Finger One. He pointed toward a tree line that ran parallel to the finger 700 meters away. A wide field of short dark grass separated the finger from the tree line. A single giant tree marked the La Tho River to the left, while a narrow canal defined the right limits of the field. My eyes fell on a small brush pile that rose out of the grass about 150 meters in front of the tree line. It was such an obvious place for a sniper's hide that I all but dismissed it.

"The only place we can figure the shots came from," the platoon leader said, "is from that tree line. Trouble is, we never know when he'll show up. He may pop off a round late this afternoon and then it'll be two or three days later, in the morning, before he comes back. He seldom misses.''

Reinke and I carefully looked over every inch of the sniper's terrain. There were so many places he could hide. But, sometimes, to paraphrase an old saying about how it takes a thief to catch one, it takes a sniper to catch a sniper.

"I have an idea that may help us locate him if he's using the same hide every time," I said.

While Reinke set up a rifle and spotting scope in a sandbagged hole and prepared to wait, I paid a visit to the Navy doctor at the aid station. I needed to do a little detective work.

"I want to know about the bullet wounds in the sniper's victims," I told him. "Can you tell me precisely where the bullets entered their bodies and where they exited?"

Next, I located witnesses to the shootings and grilled them about the exact circumstances surrounding the snipings. I was particularly interested in what the victims were doing at the time they were shot, where they were exactly, which way they were facing, and the hour of the day that they were hit.

"Well, sir, he had just turned toward that bunker there and was walking west . . . "

"Sir, he was bending over by where that truck is parked and had just straightened up . . . "

I soon developed an accurate picture of each shooting. I returned to where Reinke was patiently scanning the distant tree line.

"Anything?" I asked.

He swept his hand toward an open area to the right of the brush in the field.

"Those birds out there," he said.

A trained sniper like Don Reinke would notice details. He squinted silently into the distance. I let him proceed at his own pace.

"They've been feeding all over that field," he said. "Except for that one spot. They've avoided it all day."

I thought about it a minute.

"Let me check something," I said.

Using a map, I plotted each Marine victim's location at the time he was shot. Information about the victims' entrance and exit wounds helped me establish with remarkable accuracy the trajectory of the bullets that caused the wounds. I drew a pencil line on the map from each victim to represent these trajectories. Reinke's eyebrows lifted in surprise. The lines apexed near the brush pile in the center of the field at the spot the birds avoided in their feeding.

No one expected a sniper to be hiding in the middle of an open field. That was how he managed to escape detection.

Early the next morning, Reinke and I chanced a short recon patrol to explore the vicinity of the brush pile. Covering each other and proceeding cautiously in case the sniper had managed to slip in without our notice, the two of us stalked down the north side of Hill 55 and slowly worked our way through the underbrush until we reached the canal. Leeches resembling some kind of water plant clung to the bottom of the shallow waterway. A riot of vines, lianas, and other plant growth grappled in a wanton display of tropical fertility. We fought our way through it and crept along the edge of the field, thinking to cut the sniper's trail. The canal offered the best cover for him to reach his post.

From the hill, the grass in the meadow appeared to be the well-manicured lawn on some French estate. Down here, the reality belied the illusion. It grew knee-high in most places and up to the waist in some. It would be impossible for even the craftiest woodsman to hide his passage through it. It didn't surprise me therefore when we soon came across a faint trail of bent grass. It led away from the canal and across the field toward the brush pile.

We crouched in the growth along the canal and studied the trail and the field for several long minutes before we decided it was safe to continue. Charlie's trail in the grass led directly to the brush pile, around which the grass grew a little taller and a little thicker than in the rest of the field. Several other faint passageways converged here, indicating the VC sniper had come here more than once and by a different route each time. But the brush pile itself had not been Nguyen's destination. A tunnel through the mat of tall grass led from the brush pile toward the middle of the field.

"The gook's got himself a subway!" Reinke exclaimed in admiration.

"Let's see where it goes."

Dropping onto our bellies so as not to disturb Charlie's "subway" and tip him off, we wriggled our way forward through the grass tunnel until it ended a hundred meters beyond the brush pile in a small flattened area obviously used as a sniper's hide. From here you could see—and if you were a good shot, *hit*—anything that moved on Finger One. The sniper's frequent visits to his hide were the reason birds avoided the area. I had to admire Ol' Nguyen. Even if the Marines on the hill came to suspect his general location, they were apt to focus on the brush pile and open fire on it, leaving the sniper safe to escape and return another time.

"I think Nguyen's in for a surprise," I muttered with satisfaction.

Reinke and I worked our way back to the canal, careful to leave behind as few signs of our visit as possible. I had a plan.

"See to the left of that brush pile where you can barely see the grass looks a little different?" I asked the platoon leader on the hill, pointing.

"Yes, sir."

"Bore-sight a 106 directly on that spot. We have no way of catching the sniper until he returns and fires a shot, but when he does—fire the recoilless and see what happens."

The Marine swiveled the long 106-millimeter recoilless antitank weapon and deflected the barrel until its open snout pointed directly at the sniper's hide. The gunner slammed in an HE round and locked the breech. All he had to do was slap the push-button trigger.

Reinke wanted to stay for the action, but I pointed out we had a sniper's school to organize and supply. Besides, now that we knew Charlie One Shot's secret, the 106 could accomplish the same thing we could. Ol' Nguyen was truly in for the surprise of his life.

It wasn't long before he received it.

Late one afternoon a few days after the 106 was made ready, a shot rang out from the field. Fortunately, for one of the first times in his short-lived career, the gook sniper missed his target. The bullet gouged harmlessly into a sandbag inches behind a Marine who was darting across the open from one place to another.

While grunts either dropped where they were or leaped into the nearest bunker, the 106 gunner dashed for his weapon. He made a headlong dive for the gun's sandbagged emplacement and hit the push button. The muzzle belched a stream of flame at the field; the rocketlike backblast exploded a cloud of dust.

It was a dead center hit. Nguyen Schwartz the gook sniper disintegrated into his component parts of fingers, toes, skin, hair, teeth, and blood.

There was more than one way to get one shot—one kill.

CHAPTER NINETEEN

U.S. Marine Corporal
Ron Szpond
Vietnam, 1966

I had twelve confirmed kills and twelve probables. Two dozen of them. Twenty-four human beings. That was about like wiping out my high school home room. Snuffing out men's lives with 173-grain full-metal-jacketed bullets was what I did best in life. And it was so damn easy.

One evening, the sun was going down on Chu Lai and turning rice paddies and bamboo and Vietnamese farmers with water buffalo into one of those mysterious Oriental postcards. I slouched on the edge of a sandbagged foxhole and gazed reflectively at the scene. My thoughts weren't really on it though. My thoughts were on the Winchester Model 70 with scope that rested within easy reach, and on the .45 automatic pistol strapped to my waist and the .38 revolver in a shoulder holster. Killing so easily also made you aware of how easy it was to die.

My thoughts were on killing, and on dying. I remembered how it all began. Things would never be the same again.

"Corporal Szpond, we've gone over your records and picked you to attend sniper school up at Da Nang."

That was the company first sergeant.

"Sniper school?"

"That's right. Your rifle scores from the range and your prior experience in Vietnam make you our selection. Get your gear together and get back here as soon as you can. You've just volunteered."

That was in November 1965. I had just returned to Vietnam from lifeguarding at an officers' swimming pool in Okinawa where I went to recuperate from shrapnel wounds in my ass and left leg. My squad was running a long-range recon when we set off the booby-trap grenade. Now I was back in the 'Nam. That was the last place I wanted to be. Except the cemetery. Maybe they were the same.

A sniper, huh?

I thought about it. The gooks had killed some of my buddies. They tried to kill me. What the hell. If I had to be in Vietnam, I might as well make the time count by killing dinks. It would be different than being with the grunts where you rarely even saw the enemy. When you did see him, everybody was shooting so that you never knew who killed the one or two gooks who did fall. I could see how being a sniper was different. Killing became personal. One on one. You could get *even* with the little yellow bastards.

"I'm ready," I told the first sergeant.

Captain Bob Russell commanded the Third Marine Sniper School at the base of Hill 327. There were twelve of us from different units who made up his first class. That was about the time Lee Marvin starred in his World War II movie called *The Dirty Dozen,* so that was what we called ourselves—The Dirty Dozen. Before we started classes, we helped bulldoze ranges out of the red earth and set up targets. Then the course lasted for three days. Captain Russell issued me a new Winchester Model 70 equipped with a Unertl 8X scope and told me to go out and kill gooks.

I didn't look much like a killer when I returned to The Magnificent Bastards, which was what the Fourth Marines called themselves. I was nineteen years old, lean, with blond hair and blue eyes. But looks, I proved, could be deceiving. I was ready to kill. Primed for it. I was ready to get even.

I remember the first two I killed. You never forget the first one, but I killed two of them almost at the same time. I remember being very pleased with myself and my precision shooting.

It was December. LBJ kept promising to have "the troops home by Christmas." He never said *which* Christmas. My company commander was a captain named Gannan, a tall, thin man with a flaming red handlebar mustache. He cleared his throat.

"I want you with me in the headquarters element when we move out on this next operation, Corporal Szpond," he said. "We'll be part of the blocking force. I'll be your spotter."

A sniper team was supposed to consist of a sniper and a spotter, but men were scarce.

"I don't want anyone shooting civilians," the captain said, "but if I see we have armed VC I'll give you permission to take them out."

He studied me as though trying to decide whether or not I could do it when the time came. Dysentery had caused me to drop fifteen pounds that I really couldn't spare. My skin was leathery from the tropical sun, like everyone else's, and I was getting the so-called Asiatic stare. That's best described as a twenty-foot stare in a ten-foot room. While I might have looked like a kid, I was taking on the manner and appearance of a tough and streetwise one.

I guess Captain Gannan made his decision.

"We're moving out tonight," he said. "We'll be in position when the main sweeping force enters the village at daybreak."

By dawn I was set up with the captain on a small wooded knoll overlooking a rice field about one kilometer across. The village lay to my right front. It was checkered with live bamboo fences and paths. I thought of booby traps—Malayan gates, punji stakes, man traps, and foot traps.

The bastards.

I heard the distant chopping drone of helicopters as the sun burst bloody from its womb in the South China Sea. Long shadows were starting to finger the earth as the flock of choppers deposited the sweeping force at the far side of the village. Sporadic firing followed—Marine M-14s mixed with the sharper, shorter barks of Soviet AKs. For once, intel had hit the mark. This *was* a hostile village.

"I got two spotted at twelve o'clock," Captain Gannan said suddenly.

Eye to scope, I swung my rifle across the back side of the village.

"They're armed," Gannan said. He grinned.

The first VC filled my scope. He wore khaki and carried a pack and a rifle. He was trying to slip out the back door as the Marines came in the front.

"Take them out," Gannan said dispassionately.

The range was about seven hundred yards. I put everything I had learned about shooting into that first shot. I concentrated on the cross-hairs. The man was running directly toward me. I didn't want to blow it. I gently pressured the trigger.

The rifle cracked.

Khaki Uniform jerked in the air and crumpled to the ground. I could tell by the way he fell that he was down to stay. I switched my scope to his partner. This one wore the customary black pajamas. He panicked when he saw the first man drop. He might have survived if he had bolted either to the right or left, which would have made my next shot far more difficult. Instead, he turned and ran directly away from me. I calmly picked him up in my cross-hairs.

He didn't look back or anything. He only *ran*.

The Winchester barked.

The gook kept running.

"Goddamnit! Missed."

I worked the bolt. My second shot dropped him. His momentum carried him tumbling into the brush at the village's edge. He didn't get up.

Captain Gannan was impressed. "That's eight hundred yards!" he exclaimed.

I don't know what I expected to feel, killing my first man like that, but I blushed a little from the captain's praise. I *had* made some good shots.

"I'll get on the hook and have a squad police up the bastards," the captain said. "I'm curious about what kind of uniform that one dude was wearing and about what's in his pack."

My bullet went completely through both legs of the VC in black. It cut an artery and he bled to death lying in the bushes. The one in khaki turned out to be a Chinese advisor. Documents he carried in his pack figured in a later operation that undoubtedly saved Marine lives. I felt good about that. If I killed two gooks and that saved Marines, then *all right*. I would kill a lot of gooks.

I received a letter from Captain Bob Russell who heard about my spectacular first kills on my first operation as a sniper.

Howdy, Dinger:

Hurry back to Da Nang before we break your record and I find myself engulfed in paperwork. Here's what I need: a writer from TRUE Magazine has written to General Walt and wants to do a story of the sniper school, etc.

Accordingly, how about writing me a war novel on how you went about getting your first kills. The before, during, and after approach. You might, as a suggestion, mention very modestly that you want to revenge the piece of lead in your posterior, etc. Don't get too John Wayne-ish or I might have to get you a medal. Ha!

Just tell how it happened and I'll see that it gets to the general, via the general to TRUE Magazine. Just put yourself in the same frame of mind as a writer who writes "How I Survived Nine Days In a Cat House" or something. Need it as soon as possible, so please reply in mail. Thanks and keep your eyeball to the crosshairs.

Russell

I later learned men with a "get even" motive such as the one I possessed were rejected as sniper candidates. But this was early in the war. What the sniper program needed then were competent marksmen, not moralizers or weepers. Being a good shot was good enough.

Three magazine articles came out of Captain Russell's arrangements with the writer. They appeared in *Guns And Ammo*, *American Rifleman*, and *Leatherneck*. I read them after my war; they didn't tell how it really was. *Nothing* could tell how it really was to find yourself turning into a killer. What else could you call me? I *was* a killer. My kill score kept climbing.

I don't think anything in my previous life prepared me to become a killer. I wasn't *produced*. I *learned* to be a killer in Vietnam.

My family was very religious. I was born in 1946 in a cold water flat in Elizabeth, New Jersey, the youngest of three sons. We attended parochial school, where I came to appreciate discipline, especially self-discipline. As a post World War II baby boomer, I also learned to live with cold war events that influenced the character of an entire generation of American youth. GIs fought in Korea against the "red menace." The Russians blockaded Berlin after dividing the city with a wall and armed guards. Castro came to power and introduced communism to our hemisphere. American school children practiced air raid drills and watched films about atomic bombs and the threat of communism.

I played war with my pals, shot .22 rifles at Dutch Boy paint cans in a nearby meadow. John Wayne flew Hellcats and fought his way up Mount Suribachi. *Victory At Sea* on TV every afternoon showed how we beat the Japanese. The Bowery boys chased Nazi spies in the streets of Brooklyn.

My family was made up of warriors. Dad served as a 15-year-old lancer in the Polish army during the Polish-Russian War of 1920 before he immigrated to the U.S. and married my Polish mother. My older brother Edward joined the Marines in 1955. Brother Ray enlisted in the Marines in 1959. After my parents divorced, things at home just weren't the same anymore. I started flunking out of school. I began looking around for a place to go. The Marine Corps had provided homes for two of my brothers.

Then my mother remarried and she and my stepfather produced a blond daughter.

I enlisted in the U.S. Marine Corps when I was seventeen. Less than two years later, in July 1965, I waded the surf ashore on the sandy beaches of Chu Lai with the Ninth Marine Expeditionary Brigade.

Vietnam.

The mind finds ways of adapting when sane men are thrown into insane conditions. I adapted by making the war a personal thing. I couldn't kill *impersonally* the way it was supposed to be done. There had to be something between me and that guy out there I was about to zap. I don't think I could have killed otherwise. I had to believe that guy *deserved* killing.

The enemy made it easy to rationalize.

"Szpond, you're a wanted desperado," Captain Gannan said one day. He came up and sat down on a sandbag next to me.

"Sir?"

"We just got word from the intel folks that the VC and NVA have placed a price on the heads of American snipers. You guys are evidently pissing 'em off."

I thought about it.

"I suppose that makes me the hunted as well as the hunter," I said.

"They aren't as good as you are," Captain Gannan said. "You'll be all right. Just keep right on being a heartbreaker and a name-taker. I can't let my best shooter get zapped, can I?"

I looked at him. I was serious. "We definitely can't allow that," I replied.

I felt like somebody out there was watching me through a rifle scope. That made it easy for me to feel that I had to get *him* before he got *me*.

One afternoon I went out with a squad that was going to drop me off in a hide. Before I had time to break off, the patrol threaded up through a patch of heavy jungle and came to a bend in the trail. Suddenly, the jungle exploded in an ambush so fierce that bullets rained leaves and branches all over us. A BAR chewed down the middle of the trail. A string of flanking AKs popped like strings of firecrackers. Lead snapping past your head seemed to rob you of air.

The Marine in front of me went down hard with the first burst of hostile fire. Since my bolt-action Winchester was all but useless in a firefight, I flung it aside and grabbed the downed Marine's M-14. I joined the squad in assaulting the enemy's positions. We charged directly into the muzzle flashes. It seemed an insane thing to do, but that was *all* you could do. If you ran the other way, a mine field or a blocking force got you. If you dropped, the ambushers slaughtered you where you lay, like pigs. Therefore, you ran right at them, screaming like banshees.

It was insane.

As always, the ambushers melted away. I didn't see a single one, although I burned up a clip shooting at shadows. I returned the wounded man's weapon to him as a medevac chopper came in over the trees. He grabbed my hand and thrust something into it.

"Ron, take this."

It was his personal .38 revolver and shoulder holster that he had acquired somewhere.

"I'm being medevaced and won't need it anymore," he gasped. "Maybe it'll save your life."

Maybe it would. I slipped into the shoulder holster. I started wearing it and the .45 everywhere I went. It increased the odds of my getting *them* first.

The VC had a habit of picking up a Marine patrol in the field and tracking it until they found the proper time and place to attack it. I discovered I could turn the tables on them by going out with a patrol and then dropping off in a hide to watch our back trail. The best places to set up were in the bush just after the patrol crossed an open field or rice paddy. Using this little trick, I occasionally picked off a gook tracker as he came snooping and pooping along behind. Unless he was experienced, he generally followed the tracks across the clearing. Easy shot.

I dropped off from a squad one afternoon and burrowed into some tangled vines and lianas while the squad continued into the bush. I expected any trackers to come plowing through the elephant grass clearing that lay to my front. Instead, I hadn't been in position much more than fifteen minutes before I heard noises in the jungle to my left. I eased into a different position to meet this unexpected threat. Apparently, these particular gooks were a little smarter than the average.

Sunlight bathed the clearing, but here in the forest the gloom and the thick tangle of underbrush limited my view. I didn't dare try a move to a better vantage point for fear of being spotted. I lay with my chin in the forest humus, listening as the noises of cautious pursuit drifted deeper into the jungle on the trail of my Marine patrol.

When I could no longer hear the trackers, I considered evacuating the area. I was already easing to my feet and looking around when, suddenly, the silence was ripped apart by the nearby clatter of small arms fire. Startled, I fell flat on my face and heard and felt my heart pounding with the same frantic rhythm as in the firefight that had erupted between the Marine patrol and the band of attacking VC. The battle wasn't more than three hundred meters away. It sounded like a bunch of kids beating tin buckets inside a metal building.

My first instincts called for me to hide until the

firefight ended, then try to rejoin the patrol. Second thoughts warned me that this entire area would probably be swarming with the enemy in no time. That was enough to jerk me to my feet in a near panic. I had seen what the VC did to captured GIs—balls sliced off and rammed into their mouths. That sort of thing. I could only imagine what the gooks would do to a sniper with a price on his head.

The sounds of the fight came from my right. I started running to the left in a wide circle that, hopefully, would carry me around the VC and bring me to the Marines on their left flank. Tree branches whacked me in the face, and vines and roots grabbed my ankles as I hurtled through the forest. The jungle was so dense that I could have stepped on someone before I noticed him.

That was almost what happened. The little knot of VC—maybe five or six of them—were so intent on slipping in on the Marines from the rear that none of them heard me crashing through the trees until I was no more than ten meters away. I was so near that when I slid to a surprised halt I showered the Vietnamese soldiers with debris from the jungle floor.

None of us moved on either side for about three beats of my racing heart. We simply stared at each other like wax dummies in a wax museum. It seemed like ten minutes passed before the clatter of my useless Winchester dropping to the ground snapped the gooks out of their trance. They whirled on me with their assault rifles, but I had the jump on them. I went quick-draw style for my pistols. Clawing out a handgun with either hand, I opened fire at point-blank range. I emptied both weapons as fast as I could jerk the triggers, spraying the startled VC with bullets.

Two of them fell. The sight of a tall, blond, skinny roundeye alone in the jungle popping rounds with two little pistols must have been too much for the rest. They turned and ran. Fortunately. Both pistols were empty. I didn't stay around to check on them or the two I saw fall. I grabbed my rifle and ran the other way.

"Thank you," I whispered to the memory of the wounded gyrene who bequeathed me his .38 pistol. It *had* saved my life.

I thought about that wounded Marine now as I sat on the sandbags at Chu Lai. I wondered if he died before he reached a doctor. I kept seeing his eyes when he handed me his pistol. It was the greatest gift one soldier could give another. A tool for dealing death—but also one for saving life. It was like he knew he was giving me life when he gave me his pistol.

I mulled it over. I wasn't the type who could just *do* whatever needed to be done or accept whatever happened and then just go on and leave it at that. I had to chew around on things, mull them over, find meaning even when maybe there was no meaning.

That was what was aging me, making me an old man at nineteen. Killing others and seeing others die made you contemplate your own mortality. It had a way of making you feel old. It had a way of making you hate those who wanted to take your life from you.

Hate sustained me.

But I kept facing words from my upbringing: *Thou shalt not kill.*

Did it mean literally that? Thou shalt not *kill.* Period? Or did it mean, Thou shalt not *murder?* It was the greatest of the Ten Commandments. If you used the literal interpretation of *kill,* then I was violating it. Frequently.

But I had not *murdered.* Had I?

If I didn't kill *them,* they would kill *me.* Or they

would kill other Marines. That was what war was about, the best I could determine. You killed each other until one side got tired of being killed or ran out of people to be killed.

The most I ever hated them and wanted to kill them was when they came the nearest to killing me. That was when killing felt the most personal. Like the time NVA had me completely surrounded in a hide.

I can still see the sun hanging low above the hazy purple ridges on the western horizon. Life takes on a certain cutting intensity during times of extreme danger that condenses all your past and future into a continuing now. Your awareness triples. Life can never seem so *real* as when it faces extinction. I saw the *buttons* on the line of khaki-clad NVA that swept across the tree-dotted clearing toward me. I saw how the low sun in their faces made their skin copper colored.

Other enemy soldiers were behind me and on either flank. I was surrounded. Some farmer must have spotted me and thought to collect the reward the North Vietnamese offered for the heads of snipers. I heard movement all around me, men calling to each other. I watched the line coming toward where I lay on my belly in a briar thicket.

They were hunting me. They wanted to kill me. *Me!* I wanted to kill them in return. I could have picked off two, three, maybe even four or five. But in the end they would have gotten me and I would be *their* trophy.

That was the way it worked.

Before I entered the hide, I preselected an emergency escape route through the densest part of the jungle. I slithered out of the briar thicket and began crawling through the undergrowth on my belly. At any moment I expected to hear a cry of triumph as one of the VC spotted me, followed by the last sound I would ever hear—the burst of a communist AK-47.

I paused frequently to look and listen. I held my breath and temporarily tried to stop my heart from beating—it was so loud—at the sinister sighing of branches when a man passed nearby, at the muffled thud of a footfall, the unintentional clank of a weapon.

He was coming my way.

Using my elbows, I edged behind a fallen tree and forced my way into a mass of ferns. The odor of rotting wood and rich wet soil bored deep into my nostrils. I buried my face into the humus, leaving free only one eye which I used as a scope to peer through the ferns. That was the only thing about me that I dared move, and I moved it only slowly.

The soldier appeared. He carried his assault rifle at port arms across his chest. His finger was on the trigger. I was so scared that I actually ceased to exist when he stopped and slowly looked around. His eyes riveted on the fallen tree and the ferns. It seemed his eyes were on me for an eternity.

I knew I was a goner.

But so was he. I took what comfort I could from that, from the thought that *this* man would pay with his life for taking my life. In my mind, I rehearsed what I would do when he brought his rifle around to point it at me. I would roll to one side and as I did I would be snatching the pistols that had saved my life before.

Every nerve in my body was stretched tight enough to break. I was vibrating. I almost cried out and rolled into my plan of action when the NVA glanced away and yelled something at another gook deeper in the jungle out of my eyesight. But I held, not flushing, and that saved my life.

After another second, the gook turned and trudged on.

For an eternity more, the muscles in my body refused to respond to the frantic commands from my brain. Then they yielded. I began crawling again. Sweating from the tension, I pushed my body forward through the thickest forest I could find. Sounds of the search faded into the distant rear. Finally, I sprang to my feet and ran blindly until I knew the NVA were far behind. The breeze from running gave me a chill that I was not able to control for hours afterward.

I hated the gooks with an intense, personal hatred that consumed me totally whenever I was behind the rifle. There was always another opportunity to get even.

When NVA divisions started infiltrating out of the highlands and through the A Shau Valley into Quang Ngai province in the southern part of I Corps in January 1966, the Marines put together Task Force Delta and launched a sweep across the district. It was called Operation Double Eagle I.

My company's first objective in the operation was to clear VC out of the village of Bong Son. We came within sight of the hamlet an hour or so before sundown on January 28. The first building we encountered was a low, squat structure made of brick. The roof was flat slate. It looked like a schoolhouse.

The schoolhouse windows spat automatic weapons fire that knocked down two Marines in the point platoon. A 3.5 rocket gunner put a rocket through one of the windows. When the white-hot cloud drained out, dissipating in the slight afternoon breeze, a squad found two crispy critters inside.

Since it appeared the Bong Son VC were prepared to resist and no one wanted to be fighting them in the dark, the CO ordered the company to dig in on perimeter around the schoolhouse. I climbed to the roof with my Winchester to survey the surrounding rice paddies and the village for signs of enemy activity, thinking I might get in a shot or two before the light failed.

The terrain was ideal for a sniper. It offered long, open fields of fire all around the distant village. I nodded with approval and rolled over on one side so I could reach my canteen. The roof was still hot enough from the day's sun to make me sweat heavily. I was sipping lukewarm Kool-Aid water when two Marines ran up.

"Szpond, take a look at that shit."

They pointed at a farmer hurriedly driving his black water buffalo out the opposite end of the village. Papasan and his beast were about seven hundred yards away; they had just broken free of the last hootch and were crossing the rice paddies at a trot, using a dike trail that led to the jungle on the other side. It was obvious the farmer did not want to encounter us. My Unertl explained why.

"Well, I'll be damned."

The water buffalo had too many legs.

"Sir?" I called to the platoon lieutenant on the ground. "I got two gooks out there behind the water boo."

The lieutenant squinted across the distance.

"See what you can do to ruin their day," he said.

All *right*.

The buffalo had to go first. It went down hard on its right side with my first shot, directly on top of the weapons and equipment the fleeing gooks had strapped low on the animal's ribs. Instead of running as the farmer did, the two VC struggled frantically with the dying boo trying to retrieve their gear from

199

underneath it. I calmly cross-haired one of them and squeezed off my second round. The bullet spun the gook in a complete circle before it splashed him into the rice pond.

The second dink seemed undecided about what to do—whether to run for it, take cover, or continue to try to free his weapon. Indecision cost him his life. I nailed him permanently to the soil with my third shot.

Add two more to my body count.

I shifted on the sandbags. The Oriental scene was fading into another formless tropical night in Vietnam. Still, the thoughts of killing and dying roared through my head like a runaway amtrac on a foreign beach:

I am, in effect, playing God, in contrast to my upbringing that it is wrong to kill and all the Commandments. I realize the power that I have, being in a position to execute people. You don't have that in a regular firefight. You open up on the enemy and they fall. They are dead NVA and dead VC and everybody smiles and says, "Good, I got 'em." That isn't actually factual. The blood of the dead isn't directly on your hands.

With the precision shooting of the scoped rifle, there is no question in anybody's mind who squeezes the round off. The person falls and there's an everlasting imprint on my mind. It gives me, first, satisfaction. I recall telling the captain in a briefing that I was even for myself and now it was time to get even for the other Marines I had been personally involved with.

I am a loner full of vengeance. My desire is to even the score. I am doing this with the tool of the sniper rifle. None of the officers or NCOs fuck with me or have any reason to. I am doing my job. There is no question about that. I am very pleased with myself. I am quite pleased with my precision shooting.

I really didn't have to open up to anyone. I sometimes hear or instances are related to me where someone says, "There's the company sniper. He's kinda hard, and he's a loner." That is very true. I am a member of an elite group. Our job is to inflict as many casualties as we can on the enemy using the scoped rifle.

So here I am, a loner, with a powerful piece of equipment, full of hatred and vengeance for myself being wounded, evening the score for my fellow Marines, and having all this hatred incorporated and using it in a very sacriligeous way. There is also this intense feeling of looking death in the face, tempting fate, challenging The Reaper, so to speak. . . .

CHAPTER TWENTY

U.S. Marine Sergeant
Carlos Hathcock
Vietnam, 1967

My last sniper's mission in Vietnam was going to demand all the skills I had developed as a member of Captain Jim Land's Viet Cong Hunting Club. The five-day siege in Elephant Valley was behind me, and it had required a lot. Assassinating the Apache Woman and the French fag gave me satisfaction. But they all paled in comparison to what I was being asked to do now.

"You're the only man who can pull this one off," I was told. "We're going to be honest with you. The odds of your survival are slim to none. But if anyone can do this mission, you can."

It was a "volunteer" mission. I was almost due for rotation back to the States.

"We know you only have a few more days in-country. This is important or we wouldn't ask you. You're the best there is."

I was intrigued. They knew how to get to me. "What is the mission?"

"It's so top secret we can't even tell you until you're ready to be inserted. All we can tell you is that it's vital, and it's *extremely dangerous*. You'll have to volunteer or decline knowing no more than that. If you decline, we'll have to get someone else whose chances of success and survival are a lot less than yours."

I couldn't let someone else take a risk like that, not when it was virtually suicide. At least I had a *chance*. Besides, it was a part of my nature not to pass up a challenge.

I expected something like the French fag. That was a special, secret mission too. This Frenchman kept his plantation after Dien Bien Phu by cooperating with the Viet Minh and later the Viet Cong. The VC used his plantation as a staging point and as a safe house where they sometimes brought captured American GIs. The Frenchman helped interrogate and torture the GIs. We heard he enjoyed it.

I got him with one shot as he and some other hamburgers were walking on the road near his plantation house. He was a ton of blubber that went down to stay.

The French fag was a piece of cake compared to this one. I learned about the mission an hour before it began. I stood silently blinking for a minute. Then I slowly reached up and removed the white feather from my hat and stuffed it into my pocket. For this one I needed every advantage of camouflage and patience I possessed. If I pulled it off, I deserved the legends that went with the name *Long Tràng* given to me by the Vietnamese. If I failed, some hamburger would be collecting that reward of three years' pay the VC were offering for my head.

I couldn't help realizing that I might not be returning from this one.

"Your mission," I was solemnly told, "is to sneak into an NVA divisional headquarters, get within rifle range of the commanding general—and assassinate him."

I wasn't told why it was so vital that the general die, only that it was. I was also kept in the dark about exactly where it was I was going. "You won't need to know." For all I knew, I was going into Laos, Cambodia, or even North Vietnam. The piece of map I was given had no place names or grid coordinates on it. It and an SR-71 aerial recon photo showed a grove of palm trees surrounded on all sides by grassy, open fields at least one kilometer in width. The enemy divisional headquarters was located in an old French plantation house and another smaller building among the palm trees. The photo showed camouflaged gun emplacements scattered among the trees. I was told NVA heavily patrolled the entire area.

"A chopper will drop you and a squad of Marines off here at the edge of the map. The squad'll wait until we hear one way or another about the mission. Then the chopper will return for you."

I figured there was a spy inside the headquarters who had passed on information about the general and who would also report on the mission's success or failure.

"Let's go," I said.

I drew eighty-four rounds of match-grade ammo, my "basic load," and one canteen. That was all I needed, other than my rifle. I was traveling especially light for this one.

The squad of Marines and I boarded a helicopter at daybreak and flew for over an hour before it let down in a clearing surrounded by triple canopy jungle. Several other helicopters flew decoy insertions to throw off any observers. The other Marines accompanied me for about two kilometers before they dropped off. All the squad leader knew about the mission was that he was to wait and secure the area for my return. I would be in a hurry—*if* I returned.

Alone from there, I made my way quickly through the jungle for another three kilometers until, low-crawling the last short distance, I reached the large clearing depicted on the map and aerial photo. It was bathed in that special soft light of a late afternoon sun. I hid in the tree line and carefully studied the lay of the terrain, comparing it to the map, while I decided on a route across the open.

Grass and reeds about three feet tall covered the meadow. Its brownish-green sweep disappeared curving to both my right and left as it protectively encircled the grove of palms. The distance to the palms was about fifteen hundred meters. A white concrete house, low and rambling with wide, thrown-open French windows, squatted among the trees. Slightly behind it and to the right was the outbuilding. In front of the house was a twin .51-caliber machine gun, while other .51s protected either side and presumably the back.

Peering through my scope, I saw khaki-clad NVA doing soldierly things in the grove, while a patrol of four guards was just returning from sweeping the meadow to my left. I studied the house itself. From my briefing, I knew that the general's offices occupied the room behind the broad colonial windows to the right of the front door. The general, I had been told, was a short fat man whose habits included going out every morning to inspect the grounds and the troops. Sometimes a white Citroen parked by the outbuilding pulled up in front and took the commander out somewhere for the day. I couldn't see the Citroen from my position. Either the general was away in it, or it was parked somewhere out of sight.

The place appeared impregnable, what with the machine guns and patrols and at least a company of hard-core regulars bivouacked in the grove. Not a single tree or shrub grew in the meadow between me and the general's house. The only cover offered, I remembered from the aerial photo, was a slight depression, like a dry wash, that cut its way out of the jungle to my far right and ended in kind of a shallow bowl a little more than halfway past the center of the open field. If I could reach the bowl, I decided, I would make it my Final Firing Point. Afterwards, I would use the dry wash for my escape route. I never entered and exited a hide by the same route.

The general's habits decided for me that the best time to hit him was in the morning when he came out for his daily inspection. Shooting the general was going to stir up that place like a nest of angry wasps.

While I waited for nightfall to begin the final leg of my journey, I refreshed my camouflage face paint and prepared myself mentally for what lay ahead. I kept my mind occupied by thoughts of the job and how best to accomplish it and by observing the patrols that constantly swept the great meadow clearing.

Security seemed lax. The general must have felt safe. Guards in the grove often sat down or gathered in little clumps to talk. The meadow was too large for the patrols to cover it with any thoroughness. They often went single file in the meadow, out and back, with their weapons thrown across their shoulders like garden hoes.

None of the patrols ventured in my direction.

I was ready to go by the time the sun went down blood-red and the quick purple darkness that marks the tropics settled down gently over the clearing.

There was no moon, no wind. I took a deep breath to get rid of the ice that was trying to clog my veins. Then, dropping onto my side with the Winchester tucked against my chest, I left the relative security of the jungle and committed myself totally to the mission.

The next hours were the most important of my life, because they might be my last.

I soon established a rhythm of propelling myself along an inch at a time with one leg and my free hand. As the hamburgers were certain to have night viewing devices, I could not let them see the unnatural motion of even one blade of grass. After each painstaking movement ahead I stopped and used the toe of my boot to slowly prop up the grass my body had flattened, trying to cover as much of my trail as possible.

I measured progress in feet per hour.

I had traveled no more than fifty feet from the tree line before I heard the whispering of grasses as something passed through them. Then I felt as much as heard footfalls. I froze. A patrol was coming directly toward me. I held my breath for an agonizing time, afraid the hamburgers would hear it. I was afraid they would *smell* me. I was afraid they would *step* on me. I thought they might hear my heart thudding against the damp ground.

The shadow of a moving man loomed above the grass. I saw another to its left. They were thirty feet apart. They passed in the tall grass one on either side of me, their forms backlighted by starlight.

Others followed, a file of them on either side of where I lay helpless. They went by laughing and talking among themselves, like squirrel hunters in their own backyard. I was thankful I had taken the time to try to cover my back trail. It might have saved my life.

I inched on. Like a giant worm. A very slow worm. I traveled on my right side. I didn't dare switch to my left for fear of creating unnecessary grass movement. I kept on creeping across the meadow, inch by inch, foot by foot. It was like getting on your belly and taking half a night to crawl across your front lawn.

Sometimes I paused for a sip from my canteen. Otherwise, I intended not to eat nor sleep until this was all over. I continued the snail's pace all night and into the next morning. I depended upon the map and photo I had memorized and upon my innate sense of direction to keep me on course. I dared not lift my head above the grass to check my progress.

My luck held during the day. I crawled all day and none of the patrols came near.

The night was different. Shortly after sunset, I again heard footfalls and the grasses whispering. One soldier almost stepped on me. If he had looked down, he couldn't have avoided seeing me huddled at his feet in the gathering night. Fortunately for me, the hamburgers had not come so near during the day. It was also fortunate the hamburgers were lax; they felt secure.

Again I was thankful to have covered my trail so carefully.

If the hamburgers had only known.

That second night dragged as I continued slowly moving, inch by inch. By the time the sun rose to begin my second full day in the field, I was so weary from effort and tension that sleep threatened to overcome me. It might be a sleep from which I would not awake. Or if I did awake, it would be in enemy hands headed for interrogation, torture, and ultimately death.

When I came to the thicker grass, I let myself doze off for a minute or two at a time. I held my head off the ground a couple of inches and closed my eyes. My chin striking the ground awoke me.

The only thing that kept me going was knowing that I was drawing near my Final Firing Point and should reach it sometime during the night, in time to prepare for a morning shot. Several times I chanced taking a glance toward the house just to check myself. The nearer I came to the time and place for the general's reckoning, the more critical things became. In another day, if I weren't stopped, the general would be a fat old *dead* man.

Inch by inch.

It was a rhythm.

Inch by inch. Hour after hour. The hard sun beat down, sapping me of energy and drive. Sweat seeped from every pore of my body. I sucked sparingly at my canteen. It was almost empty.

My face was so near the earth as I crawled that it restricted my view to a foot or two ahead. It also put my eyes on a near level with a green bamboo viper that came slithering through the grass. When it sensed me, it stopped abruptly with a little startled coil of muscle, and its wicked head shot aloft. We were only inches apart as its black forked tongue tested my scent and its ruby eyes stared coldly into mine.

My pores exploded with sweat. A bite from this snake meant quick and sure death. I willed my eyeballs not to move for fear the creature would think them prey hiding in the camouflaged confines of my painted face. It took every ounce of willpower I could muster not to jump up and run.

The irony of having come this far to be stopped by a serpent!

The heavy triangular head appeared too large and heavy for the slender emerald body. It swayed slightly to the left and right, the quick oily shadow of its tongue probing. It could easily strike me. The cheek, the nose, *the eye itself*.

I dared not move. If I moved and the snake didn't get me, the hamburgers would.

The impasse continued for what seemed like hours. Then, apparently satisfied that I posed no threat and was too large to eat, the snake flickered its black tongue a last time, dropped its head, and whisked silently away through the grass.

My body collapsed. It took several minutes to settle my nerves so I could continue.

I welcomed the coming of what would be, one way or another, my third and last night in the field. Crawling through the moonless dark, I worked myself forward until my leading hand found the edge of the depression from which I would deliver the general's fatal bullet. I eased into the crater. It was only about six inches deep, but it was wide enough for me to lie in.

So far, so good. Now, if only some patrol didn't stumble upon me before daybreak, which was still a good seven hours away, and if only the general kept to his schedule.

It was the longest night of my life. I could do nothing now but lie waiting for the good shooting light of morning. I tried to rest, sleeping in that awkward way with my chin off the ground.

Once, I heard a patrol, but it passed and I did not see the soldiers. It was not until the eastern sky behind me began to pale into the shell colors of my third morning stalking the general's headquarters that I began to feel I might actually carry this thing off after all. As more light brought objects into view, I unfolded an OD handkerchief-sized cloth and laid it down so the weapon's muzzle would not kick up dust when I fired and give me away. I checked the Winchester for clogged dirt or grass. Then, satisfied that the scope was correctly adjusted and that a round was chambered and the rifle ready to go, I forced myself to relax while the eastern sky oranged and reddened and yellowed.

Presently, enough light existed for me to see the general's headquarters. I watched through the scope as the camp began to stir. Patrols drifted in and others went out. One followed the road that shot out across the field to the left of where I hid before it took to the meadow. Another left the palms and headed directly for me.

No! I was too near accomplishing my mission. Crawling across the field in the sun hadn't stopped me, nor had other patrols, nor the snake.

The grass here in the depression was shorter than in the rest of the field. If the hamburgers kept coming, they couldn't help seeing me. Alternative plans raced through my mind.

I swung my scope and settled it on the general's windows, knowing from my briefing that he was an early riser who got directly to work. Someone had thrown his window sashes wide to catch the cool morning breeze. I caught glimpses of him inside getting dressed while aides and couriers were coming and going. I considered trying to nail a vital piece of his ample torso as he dressed, then kicking over a couple of the hamburgers in the patrol before I made a break for safety during the confusion.

Even as I considered it, I knew it was foolhardy. The advancing patrol would pinpoint me with the first shot I fired. The NVA had vehicles. I didn't stand a prayer of escaping if they knew where I fired from.

It came down to which was the more important— saving my life or killing the general? Killing the general meant saving the lives of many Marines.

I was looking for the general to show enough of himself that I could make my sacrifice worthwhile when the oncoming patrol unexpectedly veered away. It took me another minute or two to believe what I was seeing. I eased loose on the trigger. The enemy soldiers slogged off across the meadow north of the palm grove, soon disappearing.

I barely had time to congratulate myself on my continuing good luck before the activity picked up at the general's headquarters. Someone drove the white Citroen around from the back and parked it in front. That meant the general was getting ready to go somewhere.

The morning was cool with a very light, variable wind. The range was about seven hundred yards, far from the longest shot I had ever made. The light couldn't have been better. There was no morning fog or mist to create distortions.

While I waited for the general to come out of his house, I mentally pulled myself into my "bubble" where nothing could distract my concentration. Inside the bubble I felt neither hunger nor thirst nor weariness. Even the chill I had felt earlier from tension disappeared. I knew I would get only one chance. I wanted to make it count.

Presently, the Citroen driver got out, opened the car door, and stood ready for the general. Other lower-ranking officers bustled about self-importantly. I blinked patiently through the eight-power scope. At this point I could foresee nothing in the world stopping me from getting my one shot.

The general came out onto the little front porch. His cap and his shoulder epaulettes sparkled with red and gold. He was a smaller man than I anticipated, and even fatter. He looked like someone had stuffed him into his khakis. He bulged at all the wrong places. As

I watched through my rifle scope, biding my time for exactly the right moment, the general yawned mightily and stretched himself in the morning sunlight.

I lowered the cross hairs to the officer's heart. I had already computed the exact range, using the map and recon photo. I took a deep breath, let half of it out, held the rest, and was squeezing the trigger, caressing it, when the general's aide stepped in front of him.

Damn! I eased off the trigger.

A moment later, the aide stepped out of the way. My scope picture again filled with the General's broad tunic and his rows of medals. This time I didn't hesitate. The rifle jarred against my shoulder. I brought it out of recoil and saw that the general was down and not moving. That meant a clean kill, a heart shot. The other NVA officers and aides were scrambling for cover. It was obvious they didn't know where the shot came from.

I had actually done it—killed the general!

No time for celebrations. While it took me three nights and two days to crawl no more than one thousand meters to get into position, it took me less than ten minutes to scramble down the gulley to the tree line. I looked back once, saw that the palm grove remained in a state of confusion and that no one was pursuing me, then turned quickly and ducked into the jungle. An hour later, I met my security patrol deep in triple canopy jungle. The patrol leader was already radioing for immediate extraction.

"We gotta get you outta here!" he exclaimed. "Recon has tapped all the NVA phone lines. They say the wires are buzzing."

He slapped me jubilantly on the back.

"Do you know what you did? You killed a general! We knew it as soon as the hit went down and recon got us on the hook. All hell is breaking loose, they said. You did it, Sarge. Goddamnit, you *did* it!''

He looked at me.

"And you made it back," he added in a softer voice.

I took the white feather out of my pocket and stuck it back into the band of my bush hat.

CHAPTER TWENTY-ONE

The heavy military six-by lurched to a halt across one of the powerline paths that cut through wooded areas of the U.S. Marine Corps Scout/Sniper School, Quantico, Virginia. Out of the truck piled two dozen of the most tattered-looking Marines imaginable. The Ghillie Suits they wore—long strips of brown-and-green burlap dangling everywhere from their field uniforms and headgear—made them look like huge clumps of dried weeds. Anything but attractive, Ghillie Suits break up the human outline and blend with the terrain, an idea in camouflage the Marines picked up from the British Royal Marines, who borrowed it originally from old Scottish gamekeepers.

Although the war in Vietnam had ended more than a decade ago and the actions in Grenada and the tragedy in Beirut were nothing but a memory of glory and a bitter memory, respectively, they had all contributed to a renewed high-level interest in preserving the art and science of the military sniper. After previous wars, when snipers were no longer needed, they were often maligned and looked upon with suspicion and fear. After all, bushwhacking was an ungentlemanly way to conduct war. Vietnam helped dispel that image. Sniping was neither cowardly nor unfair, as men like Ron Szpond, Carlos Hathcock, and Jim Land showed. It was simply an effective way of doing battle. It was used to a limited degree during the invasion of Grenada and much more extensively by Marines in Beirut.

Both the U.S. Army and the Marine Corps established permanent scout/sniper schools following the proven effectiveness of snipers in the rice paddies and jungles of the "limited" war in Vietnam. The Marines in Ghillie Suits piling off the six-by at Quantico were proof of the importance the military had finally placed upon selective marksmanship. Snipers had at last become part of the TO & E (Table of Organization and Equipment) of a combat-ready military force. No longer were prospective snipers chosen when they were needed merely because of their scores on the boot camp rifle range and then thrown unprepared into a very personal kind of combat. Sniper training in the Marine Corps lasts eight weeks, twelve to fourteen hours a day, six days a week.

The Marine sniper students at Quantico were about to conduct a *stalk,* one of the toughest phases of a course that has been called the toughest training in the Corps. During the stalk, students crawl, slither, or otherwise traverse about eight hundred yards across a field covered with low brush, then set up and fire two blank rounds at a target—without being detected. They must complete nine stalks successfully before they graduate and deploy into the Fleet Marine Force.

Gunnery Sergeant Paul Herrmann, the school's NCOIC, had been training scout/snipers since 1977.

He explained the concept of the stalk and what it was meant to accomplish:

"The most dangerous thing a sniper can face in the field is another sniper because a sniper knows just what to look for. Our students are facing two trained snipers (school instructors), who act as observers during the stalk. The students are heading toward the observers, down a channeled area, from a known distance. They have a four-hour time limit during broad daylight.

"Coming to within two hundred yards of the observers, who have high-powered spotting scopes, the students must set up, fire a blank round at them and then wait. If the observers can't see where the first shot came from, then the student fires again. If his position isn't spotted by then, the student had made a "possible" kill on that stalk. That's very rare, especially in the first weeks. The other instructors and I pride ourselves on being good observers.

"In a real situation, of course, the sniper would never come that close to a target. But we believe if they can set up on us, with the deck really stacked against them, they can set up on anyone."

The U.S. Marine Corps Scout/Sniper School was the first *permanent* facility in U.S. history established to teach combat snipers. Most experts consider it the best in the world. When the U.S. Army got around to opening its own school, it modeled it after the one at Quantico. It is doubtful if either snipers or the schools that train them would have become a part of any branch of the military if it hadn't been for Marine Captain Jim Land, who started the sniper program on Hill 55 in Vietnam. Land, like USMC Lieutenant Claude N. Harris who operated the Green's Farm sniper school during World War II, believed firmly that, as Harris often said, "Snipers can save a country." Snipers, Land said, could especially make the difference in the kind of limited warfare in which the American military was likely to be engaged in the foreseeable future.

After Vietnam, Land refused to give up hopes of founding a sniper school that would operate in peacetime as well as during times of war. In 1976, Land, by then promoted to major, held down the marksmanship desk at Headquarters Marine Corps. One morning late that year Land telephoned Major Dick Culver, also a competitive shooter and marksman whom Land had known professionally since Vietnam. Culver was then doing a tour at Haskell Air Force Base as an exchange officer working with the Air Force on an automated intelligence system.

"This is Jim Land," a gruff voice announced when Culver answered the ring. Land had a pointed dead-ahead manner to go with the bulldog set of his jawline. "Would you be interested in going to M.T.U. (Marksmanship Training Unit at Quantico)?"

Culver didn't even have to think about it. *"Yes!"*

A combat-experienced force recon officer, Culver, like Land, held a keen interest in both marksmanship and sniping. Many of his military assignments were in the shooting and combat field. He had formed a sniper platoon for the Fourth Marines, commanded the Raider School in Okinawa, and was the executive officer of the rifle range at Camp Lejeune. He had also done tours as an ordnance officer engineer and as operations officer for the Third Division. A degreed engineer, he specialized in optics, as in rifle telescopic sights.

"There was no sniper school at the time," Culver remarked privately. "I always suspected Jim Land snatched me down to the M.T.U. because he wanted a school developed."

His suspicions proved correct. Early in 1977, the two men met with high-ranking officers at Headquarters Marine Corps where they boldly proposed that regimental commanders send them Marines to be trained as snipers. When the Commandant of the Marine Corps bought the idea of establishing a sniper school, Land started the same way he had in Vietnam—by selecting instructors from the most experienced former snipers he knew. The first man he called was Gunnery Sergeant Carlos Hathcock, regarded by the USMC as its most effective and knowledgeable marksman. Land wanted him for the school's first NCOIC.

There were some fears that Hathcock's failing health might prevent his accepting the job. After his first tour of Vietnam duty ended in May 1967, he served with the M.T.U. and the Marine Corps Rifle Team until May 1969 when he returned to Vietnam as platoon sergeant of the Seventh Marine Regiment's Sniper Platoon, again on Hill 55. Whereas Hathcock seemed to have led a charmed life on his first tour, his second tour was beset with misfortune.

On August 13, 1969, he came under fire from elements of the Second NVA Division near Dodge City in Arizona Territory, where he was wounded for the first time by small arms fire. He had barely recovered from that when, slightly over a month later, on September 16, an amphibious tractor with which he had hitched a ride on Highway 1 struck a mine and was demolished. Seven Marines lay unconscious atop the burning amtrac. True to his nature, Hathcock threw the other Marines to safety before he jumped free himself. The act of heroism cost him second and third degree burns over most of his body. He was in the hospital for one year and required thirteen skin graft operations.

His injuries virtually ended his hopes for any future rifle championships, although he continued to try. Much of his body could not sweat because of the burn scars. Often, he had to be carried away from the firing line, bleeding from where his inflexible scar tissue had broken open from the pressure of his shooting jacket and sling, fainting from heat sickness.

His health received a further devastating blow when he was diagnosed in 1975 as suffering from multiple sclerosis, an incurable and increasingly debilitating disease. He was on special limited duty status when Major Jim Land telephoned him with his NCOIC proposition early in 1977.

"I wanted it," Hathcock said with the same determination that made him Vietnam's legendary *Long Tràng*.

Hathcock became more than just an instructor and the school's ranking enlisted man. He was an inspiration to students and living proof of what could be accomplished with proper training, equipment, and leadership. He quickly became a key member of the little group of Marines—Jim Land, Dick Culver, Jack Cuddy, Ron Macabee, and Carlos Hathcock—that wrote the first teaching materials used in the school. Much of the material was based directly on Hathcock's combat sniper experience and his knowledge of field crafts, hunting, and camouflage. The group also began developing what would become known as the world's finest sniper rifle.

"We did everything from scratch," Dick Culver said. "We built the facility as time allowed, built our own training aids, and did a lot out of our hip pockets with our own money."

The first sniper class went through the course in June 1977. From the sound beginning given it by Land, Culver, and the others, the school gradually evolved its courses through a succession of other commanders and instructors to the present eight-week course that is open to all Marines in an infantry slot, from private through the rank of captain, as well as to men in the other military branches and to an occasional FBI tactical element. The school runs two classes a year, one in the spring and one in the summer, turning out about forty-five graduates each year.

The founders of the unique school deliberately built a great deal of stress into the course to weed out those who made it through the initial selection process but who were subsequently considered unfit. Land all too clearly remembered Corporal Robert M. on Hill 55 who went catatonic after he was unable to cope with having killed enemy soldiers. Better, he felt, that an individual's weaknesses be discovered in training and the individual academically eliminated than to wait for the more rigorous and deadly elimination of combat.

"They're already good Marines or they wouldn't be here in the first place," explained Captain Tim Hunter, a 1984 commander of the sniper school, "but we make the course stressful. Being a scout sniper is an extremely stressful business. The school shows us how a future scout/sniper will act and react under pressure. If he can't handle the stress in a school situation, there is no way he will be able to cope with it on the battlefield."

The sniper student's academic load in the course consists of mission planning, map reading, optics as they apply to telescopic sights, the use of fire support, sniper employment, and intelligence gathering. One drill is intended to sharpen the student's powers of observation. Instructors partly conceal military objects in a room or field—anything from grenades and maps to weapons and pieces of uniforms—and have the students try to spot them.

In another drill, instructors display a variety of miscellaneous items on a table and let students study the arrangement. Then the students are taken to another room and asked to reconstruct from memory a list of the objects and their location on the table. Instructors may ask them such questions as how many keys were on a particular ring or the brand of a single cigarette.

"Field skills" include the practical application of everything the sniper needs to know to stalk an enemy, assassinate him, and then escape. The students are taught to operate in two-man teams, one acting as an observer, the other as a sniper. They learn the use of standard equipment they will need in the field—the 20X spotting scope that enables them to gauge the wind and detect targets, the FM radio with which they can call in support ranging from mortars and artillery to helicopter gunships. They practice individual movement, observation techniques, camouflage, land navigation, range estimation, and marksmanship. The nine stalks help measure the students' progress and their capabilities.

Major Dave Willis, commander of the Quantico rifle range, was asked to participate in an exercise by attempting to locate students who had constructed hide holes in which they could remain concealed for long periods of time. He first tried finding the hidden students with binoculars from four hundred yards away. When that failed, he moved forward to a position within twenty-five yards of some of the students. Still unable to find them, he was surprised that the young snipers had left no telltale signs, such as footprints or displaced vegetation, to give them away.

"I knew they would be well hidden," he said, "but it didn't realize they would cover their overhead positions so well, or that they would burrow in under stumps. I don't think many other people without prior knowledge of their positions would have found them either."

Although in recent years confidence builders such as a combat pistol course with the .45 automatic, a *quick kill* course with the M-16 rifle, and hand-to-hand combat and knife fighting classes have been included in the instruction package, precision shooting with the Marine Corps new "super rifle," a converted Remington 700 bolt-action rifle in .308 caliber dubbed the M-40A1, remains the mainstay combat weapon of the Marine sniper. Shooting begins in the first week of the course. Before a sniper graduates, he will have fired more than one thousand rounds at still and moving targets from ranges of 300 yards to 1,000 yards.

The Marine snipers are taught to practice for and achieve according to the motto: *one shot—one kill.*

More than a school for future combat snipers, the Quantico school also trains future sniper instructors since each Marine division now has a scout/sniper school of its own. Graduates of Quantico either become divisional sniper instructors or they serve in one of the eight-man scout/sniper teams that are now part of an infantry battalion's intelligence section. Marines refer to the snipers as the battalion commander's trigger finger. This "trigger finger" was well utilized during the Marine sojourn as peacekeeping forces in Lebanon.

That snipers have won acceptance as an important part of the U.S. battle team can best be illustrated by the body of doctrine that has sprung up to support them. According to the *Marine Corps Snipers' Manual,* a scout/sniper is ". . . a Marine highly skilled in fieldcraft and marksmanship, who delivers long-range, precision fire on selected targets from concealed positions in support of combat operations."

More and more infantry commanders, Marine and Army, are finding uses for such a marksman. In 1985, Major D. L. Wright foresaw many of these uses in an article he wrote for the *Marine Corps Gazette:*

"Today's sniper is trained to select targets according to their value. A target's real worth is determined by the sniper and the nature of his mission. Key targets are officers, noncommissioned officers, scouts, crew-served weapons personnel, tank commanders, communications personnel, and other snipers. Only when a sniper is positively sure his position will not be exposed or detected should he fire more than three shots from any one position. He might trade his own life for an inconsequential target by putting himself in a position of a defensive firefight. Commanders should realize that the sniper team is another supporting arm to be used. They should further be aware that a normal shot for a sniper is between 600 and 1,000 yards, with 800 yards being the median range. Also, a sniper should never fire at less than 300 yards because of the danger of being spotted.

"The sniper's role will become even more significant if he is employed in terrain such as Europe or the Middle East where a large percentage of personnel targets will be at ranges greater than 600 meters—well outside the maximum effective range of most riflemen. Commanders should also realize that snipers can be used as information-gathering agents. They can be employed in offensive and defensive combat operations in which precision fire is delivered at long ranges; in combat patrols, ambushes, and countersniper operations; in perimeter defense; as outguards of combat outposts and forward observation elements; and in retrograde operations in which snipers are part of the forces left in contact. The employment of scout/snipers should be taught to leaders at all levels and emphasized in field exercises so that the scout/sniper team will be effectively used, not misused, on the battlefield.''

It is doubtful if the Marine Corps Scout/Sniper School or its counterpart in the Army will ever be a large school turning out snipers by platoons and companies. For as Captain Jim Land once observed, it requires a ''special kind of courage'' to be a sniper, a type of courage found in only a relatively few men. When the sniper goes into combat, he is pitting all his skills and his life itself in a personal contest against the enemy. From the time he is selected to the instant he squeezes off a single 173-grain match-grade boat-tailed bullet at an enemy soldier one thousand yards away, he cannot afford the luxury of carelessness. Neither can the men who train him.

Gunny Sergeant Carlos Hathcock said it best in a remark to the first Marine sniper class at Quantico in 1977.

''In this job,'' he said, ''I won't take a second-place man. Second place is a body bag.''

CHAPTER TWENTY-TWO

U.S. Marine Corporal
Tom Rutter
Beirut, 1983

By October, the BLT Building at the Beirut International Airport would be reduced to rubble, blown up along with 243 American servicemen when a raghead drove his truck loaded with explosives through the front gate. Now, however, it still stood, thrusting the solid top of its reinforced concrete above the destruction of the battle-scarred city. It had served as headquarters for the U.S. Marines' BLT 1/8 (Battalion Landing Team, First Battalion, Eighth Marines) since we landed in Lebanon in June as a peacekeeping force.

As if anyone could keep the peace in this rat's nest of Christians, Shiites, LAF, and whoever the hell else was out there running around the city shooting at each other.

Corporal Jon Crumley drew back from the spotting scope poked through one of the firing slits in the sandbags fortifying the flat roof of the four-story Admin Building at Lebanon University. He drew a sleeve across his brow. It turned dark with sweat. He relaxed against the sandbags, six deep, enough to stop an antitank rocket, and peered wistfully in the direction of the airport BLT Building a couple of miles away.

"They got air conditioning," he said. "They got a canteen with cold beer and . . ."

". . . they don't have us," I finished.

The sun beat fiercely down. Whatever breezes happened to escape Hooterville and stir the short brush in the open fields that surrounded the university were kept at bay by the sandbags. I could hear the roar of bulldozers working.

Crumley peered again through the scope.

"What the fuck are they doing?" he wondered aloud.

"Let me take a gander."

I looked out across the field of scrub brush that clung to the eroded, sandy soil in scattered clumps to where the city took up again five hundred meters away. The various fighting factions, each clinging fiercely to its own sector and greedily attempting to take more, had brought to ruin a city once known as the Jewel of the Mediterranean. Many of the high-rises were now fire-gutted hulks, pockmarked by machine gun fire and cratered by rockets and mortars. The streets were littered with burned cars, piles of rubble, road blocks, sandbagged bunkers, and hastily constructed defensive positions, among which the ordinary people tried to go about their normal affairs until the next burst of gunfire sent them scurrying for cover.

"Someone's gonna make a lot of money in the construction business if this war ever ends," was Crumley's first comment.

"You can bet they're not building a new civic center out there," I muttered uneasily as I watched the bulldozers and the ragheads working like ants all around, only the ragged field separating us.

Whatever the ragheads were doing, I had a feeling it bore ill for us. The work started almost as soon as the Israelis bowed to world pressure and pulled their tanks and guns and soldiers out of that part of the city to the west known as Hooterville. Until that happened in the riveting August heat, the fighting generally avoided our area. We snipers had little to do. The six of us assigned to the university's roof and the other ten snipers of the STA Platoon (Surveillance, Target, Acquisition) working out of the BLT Building stood watches, cleaned weapons, suntanned, played cards, and bored each other by repeating the same old stories.

"Wait until the Israelis pull out," we kept telling each other. "*We* aren't keeping the peace. The Israelis are. The Israelis got *loaded* weapons. The ragheads know they'll get their asses shot off if they pull anything with *them*."

Our orders when we clambered down the sides of the *USS Austin* onto "Mike" boats for the June landing in Beirut was not to put loaded magazines in our rifles without permission from headquarters. That order was amended a few weeks later when hostile mortar fire killed two Marines. Now, we could put in magazines but we were forbidden to chamber a round without permission.

We were a *peacekeeping* force. But the Israelis were the ones keeping the peace. No one thought to forbid them loading *their* weapons.

One night a band of Amal militia crept up one of the washouts that veined the open field between the university and Hooterville and fired a rocket at an Israeli bunker. The rocket exploded in a burst of flame that strobed the night red. Showers of sparks splashed the dark sky. We snipers not on watch went running upstairs to the roof while the security platoon took battle positions downstairs. The top of the building offered an excellent view. We watched with unloaded weapons as the Israeli soldiers shattered what was left of the night with machine guns and tank guns. They raked the field in front of us with bullets. The surviving Amal retreated like mice driven out of a burning haystack.

"Those guys don't have to get *permission* to fire," Crumley observed.

The Marines went on alert when the Israelis left. We didn't know what to expect, but we knew what *not* to expect. Peace. There would be no peace.

The LAF (Lebanese Armed Forces) rumbled in behind the departing Israelis. They had armored personnel carriers and a few tanks and machine guns. The uniformed troops stationed themselves along the streets of Hooterville to try to maintain control and keep the Christians and Moslems separated. Things rapidly blew apart. The LAF were not Israelis.

From our fortified roof we amused ourselves watching street skirmishes through binoculars and spotting scopes. Guerrillas charged wildly through the rubbled streets spraying buildings with bullets. It was soon apparent that the Amal was wresting control of Hooterville from the LAF.

Crumley and I watched two LAF APCs (Armored Personnel Carriers) lumbering slowly through the morning along the narrow street that led to an intersection at the edge of the field. We were curious about a mob of ragheads that we could see hiding behind buildings at the intersection, but which the APC crews could not see. The ragheads were armed with Soviet AK rifles and waved green-white-and-red battle flags. We had no way of warning the LAF. All we could do was watch helplessly through binoculars as the heavy vehicles approached the ambush, nosing down the street one behind the other like a pair of blind monsters.

Suddenly, the trap sprang. Guerrillas swarmed the armored vehicles like ants on sugar. You could hardly see the APCs for the bodies clinging to them. Caught by surprise, the LAF crews immediately surrendered. The APC tailgates dropped and the crews emerged in their odd-colored green uniforms with their arms raised. Even from this distance, I could tell they were terrified. They had a right to be. The militiamen pounced on them and shoved them into the middle of the street with a barrage of vicious kicks and blows.

A militiaman covered the prisoners with the .50-caliber machine gun mounted on top of the APC. I couldn't hear what was going on, but I could tell he was yelling at them by the way he was waving one arm and jerking the gun back and forth. Ragheads started backing away from the LAF soldiers. Then the soldiers started waving their arms. One of them dropped to his knees, like he was begging.

It dawned on me.

"Jesus!"

It was about to be a coldblooded execution.

"Jon, get on the hook and tell S-2 what's going down."

The scene unfolding not more that six hundred meters away mesmerized me. I couldn't jerk my eyes from it. I felt I ought to be doing something to prevent what was surely to be a bloodbath. Weren't we *peacekeepers?*

I heard Crumley's desperate voice almost shouting into the radio mike: *"Spyglass Two, this is Spyglass One, over."*

Permission or not, I had an urge to jack a round into my .308 M-40A1 and begin picking off ragheads. They

were within easy rifle range. Everybody at the intersection was waving his arms and either shouting or
pleading. If something wasn't done immediately, it
would be too late for the LAF prisoners.

*"Spyglass Two, sitrep. A bunch of ragheads with
flags and AKs just took over a couple of APCs
and—"*

Little puffs of smoke spouted from the .50's snout.
A second later I heard its steady deadly cough and the
captured soldiers started falling. A couple of them
tried to run, but they were cut down. I couldn't hear
them screaming at this distance, but I could imagine
it. The machine gun raked a path through the soldiers
and mowed them down like wheat before the knife. A
pile of bodies lay squirming in the street. The machine
gunner raked the killing field once more to make sure
the dead were really dead. The bullets geysered the
concrete and sprayed blood and gristle and flesh.

The jubilant ragheads turned toward the university
and waved their AKs and battle flags, as though sending a challenge or a promise to do to the U.S. Marines
what they had just done to the helpless Lebanese
soldiers.

I turned away from the gory scene as the ragheads
piled onto the APCs. Under different management, the
machines crawled away from the intersection and
down around a corner out of sight, leaving the dead
men lying in the street beneath the Mediterranean
sun.

"It's too late," I muttered angrily to Crumley as he
eased up beside me. He squinted disbelievingly
through the firing slit to where the executions took
place. He was sweating.

"Spyglass Two said they're Shiite militia," he reported. "They have intel reports that describe them."

I was still shook. Crumley looked pale beneath his tan.

"I wonder just how bold they'll get," I said.

It was a few mornings after that incident that bulldozers appeared and started work around the edges of our field. Reports filtered in that the LAF had abandoned Hooterville and the Amal controlled most of the city surrounding the university and the airport. Puzzled, we watched and commented and waited until it became readily apparent what was happening. Berms and bunkers and other fortifications were gradually taking form, their firing slits and gun positions all facing *toward* us at the university. We learned that the same kind of preparations were going on around the airport.

With increasing discomfort we realized that the ragheads were *fencing* us in, cordoning off UN forces into little pockets.

"I understand how future Kentucky fried chickens feel when Colonel Sanders comes snooping around," I said to Crumley.

"Rutter, you been in the sun too long. *We* have *them* surrounded."

"Wasn't that what Custer said?"

After the fortifications were completed, it became some kind of game for the Shiites to peg bullets at us at all hours of the day and night. Small groups of them would run around the edge of a building, expose themselves long enough to throw a few quick bursts, then dash for cover. Others fired at us from the fortifications, generally no more than a burst or two, before they retreated and another group stepped in somewhere else. Bullets were always zipping over our heads or thudding into the sandbags.

Although we were well out of the effective firing

range of the Amal's Kalashnikovs and the incessant picking away at us was doing little damage, it still kept us on edge. We dared not relax our vigil. For the Moslems, to die for Allah was an honor. A martyr went directly to Heaven. It wasn't beyond the terrorist mentality for would-be martyrs to come charging us across the open field.

We grew tired and frustrated. This wasn't the way Marines were supposed to fight. Rules of engagement still called for us to seek permission before chambering a round. Somebody recalled that the first troops that went to Vietnam were shackled by the same kind of rule. I didn't remember much about that. I was only about eleven when the last American left Saigon.

Although we were out of effective range for the Shiite militia, they were not out of *our* range. Zapping them at six hundred meters was an easy shot for the M-40A1. I got to picking out targets through my scope and squeezing the trigger on an empty chamber, pretending.

The Shiites grew bolder until they were rapping away at us with machine guns. We were well within a machine gun's range. We cowered behind our sandbags with empty chambers.

"The longer we take this shit," everybody grumbled, "the braver the ragheads get. We'll have 'em sitting at the edge of the campus shooting at us."

That all changed one morning when a shout came bellowing out from the Admin Building's bowels. Corporal David Baldree took the stair steps two at a time to the sandbag penthouse where we snipers had gathered to keep an eye on the ragheads. He had been on radio watch.

"*It's time* . . ." he sang out, grinning. "Looks like we finally get to play. BLT just made the decision. We don't have to take any shit anymore. From now on,

233

it's up to *us* when to fire. They shoot at us, we shoot *back*."

"All *right*."

I patted the camouflaged stock of my .308.

"Them shitbirds are in for a surprise," I said.

The sun set, flinging long inflamed streaks across the troubled skies above the besieged city. Shadows in the streets of Hooterville grew inch by inch. I had just assumed watch on the roof with Corporal Baldree and was making my first sniper's log entry after examining through binoculars the parapets and fortifications that surrounded us.

"*1730 hours*," I wrote. "*All quiet. No new obstacles or positions.*"

Baldree stood at one of the firing ports scanning his front. He looked back at me and shrugged, all quiet, as I returned to my firing post opposite his. I peered out. Hooterville was almost dark, although all the light had not yet drained out of the sky. Maybe the ragheads had already heard we had turned and were going to start shooting back.

Suddenly, a string of bullets screamed over our heads above the sandbags as a heavy machine gun opened up from somewhere at the edge of Hooterville. I ducked instinctively. So did Baldree. We grinned sheepishly at each other as the next burst of machine gun fire chewed viciously at the sandbags.

"Surprise, surprise, meathead!" I yelled at no one in particular. "We can shoot back!"

We darted from one firing port to another, taking quick looks out, trying to locate the nest. Every few seconds the machine gun snapped a few rounds at us. The rounds were hitting near the firing openings in the sandbags, but so far none of the bullets had come through. I didn't want my head framed in an opening when the gunner finally hit it.

"I don't see a goddamned thing," Baldree cried in exasperation.

"Wait . . ." I said. "Okay . . . The tall building at two o'clock. See it? Second floor. The dude knows his stuff. He's not firing from the window. He's back in the shadows."

"I see him!" Baldree hooted as quick, flickering muzzle flashes lit up the room. We were watching through scopes and binoculars.

"He's too far back in the room," Baldree said. "We can't get his angle from here."

I had a thought.

"No, but we can double-team the shitbird."

I grabbed the field phone and got Crumley who was on watch at the grunt's concrete barrier on the ground floor. I quickly outlined our plan to him. Baldree and I would mark the window with rifle tracers if the grunts would follow up with their M-60 machine gun. We finally had our chance to fight back. I didn't want our first raghead getting away.

"You'll have to be quick," I warned Crumley. "The shitbag'll probably run for it as soon as we shoot from up here."

"Can he outrun a speeding bullet?" Crumley asked.

I checked the range with the mil-dot scale in my rifle scope. It was about six hundred yards.

"Ready?" I asked Baldree.

He leaned into his firing port with his rifle. "Ready."

Two tracers streaked across the field in the gathering darkness like swift angry bees. They plunged through the enemy machine gunner's window, clearly marking it for the Marines below. Larger, angrier bees followed as the M-60 on the ground floor sent a stream of tracers through the same window. The M-60 pumped the distant room full of lead. Tracers trapped inside the concrete room ricocheted insanely in a weird kind of light-and-shadow show.

"Surprise! Surprise!" Baldree shouted in a perfect falsetto imitation of TV's Gomer Pyle.

My entries into the sniper's log for the rest of the night read simply: *All Quiet.*

Things did not remain quiet. The ragheads quickly recovered from their surprise and started pegging at us again from Hooterville and the fortifications. Although we didn't have to seek permission anymore to return fire, we were still a part of the intelligence network and kept BLT headquarters informed.

"Spyglass Two, we got incoming fire, over."

"Roger, Spyglass One. Can you suppress?"

Could we suppress?

Sporadic firing was coming from several of the berms and bunkers that surrounded us. I radioed the line company Marines below and asked them to send up the other STA guys.

"We have targets," I informed them.

I knew that would bring the other snipers running. They scrambled upstairs, took their places at firing points, and began pinpointing target locations. The sun beat down fiercely. Sweat stung my eyes. I wiped it away as I tried to focus on one of the enemy skirmishers who was playing hide-and-seek with us from behind a berm six hundred meters away. His head poked up from one end of the berm and he fired a couple of quick rounds, then reappeared again at the other end of the berm to burn off another round or two.

"I'll keep an eye on that asshole until I can get a shot," Crumley suggested. "See if you can find another."

I concentrated through sweat on the shattered city as I swept my cross hairs across it. I stopped when I saw a muzzle flash blossom from the darkened revetment of a sandbagged bunker at a street intersection. The bunker's firing port was a rectangle about six inches by a foot in width. I waited until the muzzle flashed in it again before I sent a single 173-grain bullet through the tiny opening.

No more firing came from that location.

Could we suppress?

While I was busy with the bunker, Crumley was still playing cat-and-mouse with the raghead behind the berm. I scoped over to it. The raghead might think he was the cat, but we knew better now. He had made a mistake in establishing a predictable pattern. First, he fired from one end of the berm, then ran to the other end to fire. Back and forth. Crumley zeroed in his scope at the berm's near end and waited. The raghead was the mouse. Sooner or later, the cat caught it.

"He's mine," Crumley announced calmly while I watched through my scope.

"He's yours."

Thoughts of the LAF executed in the street flashed through my mind; I was satisfied that one of the killers was about to get his just reward.

The skirmisher was wearing a patterned turban. He stuck it and his head up once too often. Crumley was ready. He fired. The high-powered bullet kicked up dirt in front of the man's face. At the same time, his face underneath the turban literally exploded.

We waited, but there was no further incoming fire.

Could we suppress?

A few minutes later an old red-and-white ambulance raced up the street and stopped by the berm. Two men jumped out and tossed the dead raghead into the back. Neither of them so much as glanced at the university. They got back into the ambulance and raced off again.

CHAPTER TWENTY-THREE

The statistics of the U.S. Marine Corps M-40A1 Sniper Rifle sound impossible. It launches a 173-grain projectile at 2,550 feet per second, arching fifteen feet in the air for almost two seconds, the time it takes to recite "Now is the time for all good men to come to the aid . . ." to hit the precise center of a man's chest one thousand yards away—a distance of over one-half mile.

The rifle was not developed overnight. The development of sharpshooting has followed the development of the rifled barrel and the improving technology of ballistics, optics, and machining. Special marksmen from the Revolutionary War through every war fought by Americans, up to and including the "peacekeeping" forces in Beirut, have proved capable of extending their killing power three to ten times the range of the ordinary infantryman. The M-40A1 is simply a continuation of that progress, although many would claim it is the culmination of the sniper's skill and technology.

Two hundred years ago during the American Revolution, Major George Hangar of the British Army shook his head and complained about the quality of the firearms used by King George's men:

"A soldier's musket, if not exceedingly ill-bored (as many of them are), will strike the figure of a man at eighty yards; it may even at 100, but a soldier must be very unfortunate indeed who shall be wounded by a common musket at 150 yards, provided his antagonist aims at him; and as to firing at a man at 200 yards with a common musket, you may just as well fire at the moon and have the same hopes of hitting your object. I do maintain and will prove, whenever called on, that no man was ever killed at 200 yards, by a common soldier's musket, by the person who aimed at him."

Accurate rifles with greater ranges *were* available during the Revolutionary War, but the tactics at the time demanded massed lines of infantry facing each other at relatively close quarters while each side attempted to overwhelm the other with a "wall of flame and lead." The British musket, called the Brown Bess, as well as the hunting and fowling pieces of the colonists, were mostly smooth-bore flintlocks or, in some cases, wheel locks. Accuracy with these weapons in battle was not necessarily expected. They simply put out so much lead at one hundred yards or less, like throwing handfuls of shot, that some of the balls were bound to find a target. Firefights were much like that in Vietnam, although the M-16 is extremely accurate out to its maximum effective range of 350 yards. It was just that so few soldiers were capable of firing it accurately.

One colonist during the War for Independence who understood the musket's limitations and the shortcomings of the European style of stand-up shoulder-to-shoulder tactics was Charles Lee, an English convert to the patriot cause who had had experience with the British Army fighting the French. Lee attended the meeting of the Second Continental Congress in Philadelphia a month after the first day of fighting at Lexington—273 British casualties, less than 100 minutemen—which formed a Continental Army and named George Washington as its commander-in-chief. Charles Lee was awarded the rank of Major general. He immediately recommended that the frontiersmen of Virginia and Kentucky be recruited in the fight.

"The frontier riflemen will make fine soldiers," he argued, extolling "their amazing hardihood, their methods of living so long in the woods without carrying provisions with them, the exceeding quickness with which they can march to distant parts, and, above all, the dexterity to which they have arrived in the use of the rifle gun. There is not one of these men who wish a distance less that 200 yards or greater object than an orange. Every shot is fatal."

The rifle Lee was talking about in the hands of these frontiersmen was the so-called Kentucky long rifle or American long rifle. It went by several other names as well, since it was widely manufactured by frontier gunsmiths. But whatever it was called, it was, like the colonists, an import from Europe.

The long rifle was a copy of the *jaeger* rifle developed and used by the gamekeepers, foresters, and hunters of central Europe from the early 1600s. It was conceived as a big-game rifle for shooting deer and wild boar. *Jaeger* means "hunter" in German.

Rifles before the *jaeger* had used a wheel lock and a light, straight butt stock designed to be held against the cheek when firing. Seeking greater range and accuracy, European hunters gradually modified existing rifles. They progressed to the broad butt stock for bracing against the shoulder, making the resulting weapon more stable and therefore more accurate. They discarded the wheel lock in favor of the new French flintlock. The flintlock did not ignite quite as quickly as the wheel lock, but it could be fired faster and was simpler and much cheaper to make and repair.

Over the years, the rifle that became the *jaeger* developed other distinctive features. It was short, with an octagonal barrel averaging between twenty-four and thirty inches in length. Its bore was large, usually between .60- and .75-caliber, giving it real stopping power. Deep rifling multi-grooved for accuracy and well-designed open sights permitted a skilled marksman to fire tight groups at ranges of two hundred yards or more.

Designed as a sporting arm, it nonetheless quickly entered the military field. King Christian IV of Denmark armed some of his troops with *jaeger* rifles early in the 1600s. Norwegian ski troops were equipped with *jaegers* in 1711. The idea spread. The rifle soon became standard for all Germanic countries.

Settlers from Germany and Switzerland brought the *jaeger* with them to Pennsylvania early in the 1700s. The gradual lengthening of the barrel and lightening of the stock soon created the famed American gun used with such deadly accuracy by the frontiersmen.

General Washington was less than enthusiastic about General Charles Lee's suggestion to include the frontiersmen and their long rifles in his army. While acknowledging that the frontiersmen were fierce fighters in the Indian style, he expressed reservations about them because it was well known they were anything but sticklers for the discipline an army required. Washington was afraid their independence and quick tempers would be disruptive.

Congress nevertheless approved General Lee's recommendations. Colonel Daniel Morgan recruited one of the first bands of frontier riflemen out of the wilds of Virginia and Tennessee shortly after the Battle of Bunker Hill. General Lee watched with growing excitement a test Morgan devised to demonstrate his new soldiers' competence in weaponry.

He outlined a man's nose in chalk on a board and nailed the board to a tree sixty yards away. While the townsmen and farmers gathered to watch, the frontiersmen in their hunting shirts and buckskins stepped up to the firing line one by one. The first forty shooters obliterated the nose. By the time the entire company had shot, nothing remained of the board except splinters. Every man passed the test.

"Send the splinters to King George!" a shout went up. "Let him know the mountain boys are after *his* nose."

The marksmen of Morgan's special regiment could place a ball on a man-sized target at ranges of 300 to 400 yards, a feat unheard of by most European standards. The *average* rifleman among them could hit an enemy in the head at 200 yards. Yet, it was as Washington feared. The frontiersmen were an unruly lot. Hardly had they set up their camps than they began to slip away into the woods in ones and twos to stalk the British who still held Boston. They saw their duty as killing British soldiers in the same manner as they and their fathers had fought Indians.

They hid in the woods and picked off targets of opportunity. They popped a round at any Redcoat they spotted, at whatever distance, often connecting. Shots ringing out unexpectedly from great distances were both surprising and demoralizing to the British.

General Washington, however, was like virtually all military men of the era, and many into modern times. He did not understand sniper tactics and therefore disapproved of them. Before the sniping could have any real effect, Washington grew tired of the endless pop-pop and gave stern orders on August 4, 1775, against "futile firing."

Although the "shirtmen," as the frontiersmen became known because of their hunter's shirts, continued to use Indian tactics against the British for the rest of the war, few military men on either side of the conflict recognized the value of snipers and long-range shooting.

One of those who did was a Scottish captain named Patrick Ferguson whose development of a new, more accurate rifle added to the advancement of long-range shooting.

It was a stormy afternoon in June 1776 that Ferguson introduced his rifle to members of the British War Office gathered on a field outside London. The gentlemen milled, waiting for Ferguson's demonstration. Few believed Ferguson could do what he claimed with the rifle he designed himself. Even a skilled infantryman could not fire more than two or three shots a minute, and men and officers alike felt safe from musket fire beyond two hundred yards.

Eyebrows lifted as the Scottish captain paced off two hundred yards across the grass and propped his target against a tree. He carried a strange weapon in his hand.

"You propose to strike *that*," said a disbelieving cabinet officer, pointing at the distant target, "with *that?*" pointing at the strange rifle.

The members of the British War Office chuckled condescendingly. Ferguson merely smiled as he passed his weapon to the spectators for their examination.

The rifle was a breechloader, the first the ministers had ever seen. An extended trigger guard unscrewed a full turn to drop a threaded trapdoor to accept charge and ball on the top of the breech end of the barrel. It had a rifled barrel molded after the *jaeger*.

Black clouds scudding across the sky, pushed by gusts of wind, hurried the ministers in their inspection of the weapon. One of them said impatiently, "Let's continue with this before we are all soaked."

Captain Ferguson asked that he be timed. He quickly loaded the rifle and stepped to the firing line. The clock began. He ignored the rising wind and the threat of rain as he sighted, fired, and reloaded. At the end of one minute, he had fired five times, nearly twice as fast as any infantryman with a musket.

And with a great deal more accuracy. He had—at two hundred yards!—struck the target all five times.

The members of the British War Office fell into stunned silence. They watched intently as Ferguson increased his rate of fire to six shots a minute and delivered thirty balls as fast as he could squeeze the trigger and reload. He missed the target only three times.

The British War Officers cheered.

Four months later, Ferguson demonstrated his rifle to King George at Windsor Castle. Impressed, the king asked at what speed Ferguson could fire if he were in a hurry.

"Seven shots a minute, Your Majesty, but at that rate I can only be sure of killing five of Your Majesty's enemies."

Ferguson's rifles made their first impact at the Battle of Brandywine Creek on September 11, 1777. Maneuvering to occupy Philadelphia, Howe's Redcoats clashed with Washington's troops on the creek outside town. Ferguson's company on one flank opened withering fire at ranges that had previously been available only to the American frontiersmen. More than one thousand colonists fell casualty to British fire. Their bodies littered the field. Some of the Americans had been hit as far back as three hundred yards from the British lines. It stunned even the shirtmen.

Just before the battle began, Captain Ferguson received the opportunity to change the course of history. He drew bead on a rebel officer wearing a tricorner hat and riding a horse, but he would not shoot a man in the back. His prospective target was George Washington.

Ironically enough, Captain Patrick Ferguson, an advocate of accurate, long-range rifle fire, was killed at the Battle of King's Mountain while fighting another proponent of the same theory—Colonel Daniel Morgan and his shirtmen. With Ferguson's death, the British placed the rifles he developed in storage. Colonel Morgan's tactics and strategies had never been taken too seriously by the colonists either. The philosophy of *one shot—one kill* went dormant in America, at least as far as the military was concerned, until Andrew Jackson dusted it off at the Battle of New Orleans and, again, until the American Civil War when snipers on both sides took a dreadful toll.

The common issue infantry weapon at the beginning of the Civil War was a smooth-bore muzzle loader with a maximum effective range of 150 to 200 yards, not much better than the British Brown Bess or the muskets of the average colonist nearly a century before. However, it wasn't long after Bull Run before officers on both sides saw the value of snipers.

Colonel Henry Berdan enlisted the support of General Winfield Scott to raise two regiments of sharpshooters for Union forces. He armed them with the Sharps breechloading rifle that owed its design to the Ferguson rifle of 1776. The Sharps in .45 or .50 caliber had adjustable iron sights and was remarkably accurate. Using hand-carved wooden rear sight extensions, snipers were known to have picked off enemy targets at one thousand yards, thus matching the skills of modern snipers equipped with 10X scopes, tested match-grade ammo, and hand-machined weapons.

Snipers were used at virtually every major battle by both the Blue and the Gray. They were used on both the offense and the defense in much the same way they were used later in World War I and World War II. No slouches themselves when it came to pinpoint shooting, the Confederate snipers proved themselves at places like Devil's Den where they systematically picked off Union officers at long ranges.

After the Civil War and past the turn of the century, the U.S. Army equipped itself with a rifle known as the Krag-Jorgensen, adopted in 1892. The rifle left a lot to be desired in comparison to the rapid advancements of weaponry in the late 1800s. For that reason, the Springfield Arsenal in Illinois began manufacturing in 1903 a Mauser-based rifle modified around a new American cartridge known in military jargon as: Cartridge, Ball, Caliber .30 in M-1903. This cartridge had a blunt nose. When the Germans introduced their *spitzer* sharp-nosed bullet to better all-around performance, the Americans quickly remodified the 1903 Springfield to its classic form to accept the newer cartridge.

The U.S. Army took the 1903 to France in 1917 where it served both as an infantry weapon and, equipped with a telescopic sight, as a sniper's rifle. It remained in U.S. Army service as a sniper rifle up until after the Korean War.

The *jaeger* rifle design and the breechloader Ferguson introduced continued to be modified and improved upon to increase accuracy, range, and firing speed. The M-1 Garand made its appearance in the U.S. military in 1932. It was the standard-issue weapon during World War II and Korea. Two special sniper versions, the M1-C and M1-D, were manufactured in limited numbers in 1943. They had such extras as muzzle flash cones, butt plates, and set-action triggers.

In 1957 the U.S. Army introduced the M-14 rifle. It was a lighter version of the M-1 Garand reworked for increased ammunition capacity (eight rounds for the M-1, twenty for the M-14) and for an improved feed that eliminated the distinctive *ping!* of the M-1 clip being ejected when the last round was fired. Marines landing in Vietnam in 1965 were armed with M-14s. By the end of the year most U.S. Army units in Vietnam had switched their units over to AR-15s and then to today's standard rapid-firing M-16s. The Marine Corps did not completely switch over until 1967.

At one time or another, American snipers in Vietnam trained on and used M-1Ds, M-14s, M-21s (a sniper version of the M-14), 1903 Springfields, Winchester Model 70s, and Remington 700s. The Winchester Model 70 with an 8X or 12X Unertl scope proved a favorite with many snipers. Using 30.06 match ammo, it proved accurate out to one thousand yards.

Around 1967 Marine Corps snipers officially began using the Remington 700 with a Redfield variable 3X9 scope (called an M-40) in order to match the 7.62 ammo that was used by the M-14, still its main battle rifle. The Army at the same time turned to the match-conditioned M-14, known as an M-21 when coupled with an automatic ranging telescopic sight.

The Remington 700 had problems that made it less than the ideal sniper's rifle. It could not take the abuse a sniper's rifle needed to take in the field. The barrel was too light. Neither the stock nor barrel were camouflaged. The scope mounting could sometimes be knocked loose. The Redfield scope was not "repeatable," meaning that it could not be easily reset following a range change.

Shortly after Jim Land and Dick Culver opened the U.S. Marine Corps Scout/Sniper School at Quantico in 1977 and snipers were made a permanent part of the USMC TO & E, the Marine Corps authorized them to design a special rifle for a special job. Until that time, U.S. snipers had been using modified regular-issue infantry weapons or big-game hunting rifles.

For the first time the Marines would have a weapon specifically designed for one thing—hunting armed men, the most dangerous game of all.

The Quantico team that would design the new weapon consisted of: Culver and Land; Major Bob Faught, the Infantry Weapons Officer at Headquarters Marine Corps; CWO-4 Neil Goddard, M.T.U. shop chief at Quantico; and Gunnery Sergeant W. W. Wiseman, a former Olympic rifle team armorer.

The first thing the members of the team had to decide was whether to choose an automatic or a bolt gun. They tested the automatic feed M-21 used by the Army, concluding that self-feeding rifles have certain problems with so many moving parts. The bedding of the M-21 sometimes cracked, the receiver shifted, and the gas piston fouled. One Army sniper at Fort Bragg observed that when its rifle team traveled, the maintenance van went with it.

Maintenance problems were one thing a sniper could not afford in combat. Besides, the Marines decided they did not need the fire volume of an automatic weapon. What they were seeking was long-range precision.

After testing a number of other rifles, both automatic and bolt, the design team decided to stay with the basic Remington 700, but to modify it to meet the sniper's special needs. Using that as a starting point, the team solicited the opinions of many former snipers and match shooters to develop a rifle from a mixture of the best in bench rest guns and long-range rifles. The result after nearly two years of trial and error was a sniper's rifle known in Marine military jargon as the M-40A1.

Without its scope, the M-40A1 weighed twelve pounds, was forty-four inches long, with a twenty-four-inch stainless steel Atkinson heavy barrel set into a stock of pressure-molded fiberglass. The barrel of each gun was delivered to Marines as a blank, into which armorers cut a recessed crown, threaded it to fit the receiver, and then chambered it for 7.62 match ammo. The large diameter barrel, .960 inches at the muzzle, aided in stability.

The stock had to be as special as the rest of the weapon.

"We took a stock and modified it until it met every specification that we thought a sniper rifle should have," explained Dick Culver. "We sent it out to Gale MacMillan in Phoenix to duplicate in fiberglass with camouflage color impregnated into it."

Fiberglass stocks are impervious to heat, cold, and moisture.

"We took it out and ran over it with a pickup truck, shot at it with an M-16 and a .300 magnum, and tested it every way we could think of."

For nearly two years the original stock model was used as a "shop club" at the Quantico armory. One day Gale MacMillan visited the shop. One of the Marines demonstrated the stock's durability for the thousandth time by winding up and slamming the concrete floor with it. It finally cracked.

"Yeah, it'll break if you use it like that," MacMillan remarked. "But I'd say that that's almost Marine-proof."

The Marine armorer carefully hand-assembled the specially made parts for the first new rifle—the Packmayr recoil pad, the steel Winchester floor plate and trigger guard specially modified for the rifle, the stainless steel barrel treated to turn it a dull black, the Remington 700 receiver "glassed in" to the stock with epoxy-steel resin which won't crack, doesn't shrink, and isn't affected by cleaning solvents. The stock was attached to the barrel and receiver by Allen head torque screws to prevent shifting. Finally, the Remington trigger was fine-tuned to release at exactly four and one-half pounds of pull.

"We then put the rifle on a machine rest on the 300-yard line," Culver continued, "and fired it with the M-118 Lake City match-grade ammunition to see what it would do. It gave us a 'minute-of-angle' accuracy at 300 yards. Theoretically, it would hold a shot group inside a twelve-inch circle at 1,200 yards. We were happy."

Happy with the sniper's rifle, the design staff held a contest to select the proper telescopic sight. Redfield and Unertl were the finalists. Unertl won with a 10X telescopic sight of solid steel that weighed 2.2 pounds. The optics were thick, strong, precision hand-ground lenses coated with a revolutionary light-transmitting substance that allowed passage of 92 percent of the ambient light, compared to 72 percent for most other scopes. It was equipped with a ballistics cam cut exactly for the trajectory of the Lake City 173-grain match sniper ammo. It automatically gave the exact zero for 100 to 1,000 yards. All a shooter had to know was how tall a man should be in relation to the number of mils at a given distance.

"It's not a very pretty weapon," said Gunnery Sergeant Paul Herrmann, former NCOIC of the Quantico Sniper School, "but you can drag it through the brush and give it one hell of a beating and still hit a target at a thousand yards."

Captain Jack Cuddy didn't mince words. He called it "the best sniper rifle in the world."

At least when it comes to equipment, marksmanship has advanced a great distance from the European *jaeger* and Captain Patrick Ferguson's breechloader, although the basic concepts of both firearms are still being utilized up to the present time. Still, a hard-shooting accurate rifle is only one part of the sniper equation. The shirtmen proved that with their rather primitive long rifles during the Revolutionary War when they were able to hit targets at greater than three hundred yards. The other part of the equation, the more important part, is the man behind the rifle.

CHAPTER TWENTY-FOUR

U.S. Marine Corporal
Tom Rutter
Beirut, 1983

The sun had just risen. I was already starting to sweat underneath my flak jacket. I brimmed my soft cover low over my eyes to keep out the sun while I studied the juxtapositioning of buildings and streets that lay out ahead of Charlie Company on our side of the Beirut International Airport. The first thing that struck me was a huge likeness of the Ayatollah Khomeini covering almost one whole wall of a building facing us across a sandy open field that served as a kind of no-man's-land between the Marines and the city.

I continued studying the new terrain. Corporal Rock McGlynn and I had cut across the airport last night to join Charlie Company.

"First Platoon has been taking excessive amounts of small arms fire and RPG rockets at their sector of the airport," the intel chief briefed McGlynn and me. "There are already three other snipers along that sector. See what you can do to help them. Make sure you identify your targets, and don't make a mistake.''

First Platoon was more vulnerable than the Marines at the university. It occupied a string of ground-level sandbagged bunkers that followed a pot-holed macadam road that circled on around the airfield in a wide loop. The ragheads had already killed two Marines, one of them yesterday as he was jeeping along the road in front of Charlie Company's bunkers.

Much of the trouble originated at the mouth of a rubble-strewn street that opened directly in front of me about five hundred meters away. Jetliners followed the street to a landing at the airport behind me. They came in low over "The Danielle Cafe" in front of which a number of unarmed militiamen had gathered. The ragheads slapped their sides and hopped around a little against the morning chill. Autumn was coming to the desert.

I returned to the giant poster of the Ayatollah across the street from The Danielle. His scowling countenance overlooked a sandbagged roadblock and a bunker. His dark eyes piercing the haze of that October morning probed deep into mine. It made me uneasy. My uneasiness grew as he kept staring at me. I lifted my rifle and settled the cross hairs directly between the brooding eyes of Khomeini's giant likeness.

"*Pow!*" I said. "That's one bastard I'd like to drop."

Someone at The Danielle opened the cafe door for the militiamen. They hurried inside. After awhile, when the sun started warming things, the Amal came out armed with Soviet AKs. Their entire demeanor had changed since earlier. They knew we wouldn't shoot at unarmed men. Now, they came out running and scurried to cover behind sandbags and buildings. Sporadically throughout the day they pegged shots in our direction, but they were a lot more cautious after we started shooting back. Sometimes all you saw was an AK with a hand attached to it pop up from somewhere to blindly let off a burst, not to reappear at that same location for the rest of the day.

The ragheads had learned respect.

Silent forms sneaked back into The Danielle after dark to cache their weapons for the night, only to repeat the routine of workers-waiting-for-coffee the next morning.

The entire thing was insane, surrealistic. There was no logic or sense to it. There wasn't really a *war* going on in Beirut. It was more like anarchy in which everyone went armed. People killed each other—and mostly there didn't seem to be a purpose behind it. The only thing I could make out of it was that everybody hated everybody else for some unfathomable reason. You could see the hate in the eyes of the Ayatollah poster.

Maybe that was the point of it all—simple, casual, aimless *hate*.

"A couple of mortar rounds some morning would take care of that bunch at The Danielle," McGlynn commented, kneeling behind sandbags while he glassed the militiamen waiting for the cafe to open.

"And one thirty-six-cent bullet would take care of their beloved leader," I added.

The Shiites had their routine down. They waited outside until The Danielle opened, bunched through the door, then came running out a little while later with their weapons, which they did not discharge until they were safely behind cover. That was why it was such a surprise to us one morning when the Amal varied their routine and burst out the cafe door spraying bullets as they came.

McGlynn coolly raised his rifle.

"I'll take the first one," he said, drawing a bead on

a terrorist wearing a green uniform and a helmet liner. He was probably a LAF deserter.

McGlynn led the running target with his M-40A1, the most accurate sniper's rifle in the world, and with one shot stopped the deserter's flight across the street. The man's helmet liner exploded into the air, its wearer knocked out from underneath it, the 173-grain bullet striking the militiaman's face with the same effect as shooting a watermelon with a shotgun.

The Shiite collapsed on top of his rifle. Many men kicked and flopped around when they got shot in the head, but this one did not move. His helmet liner fell on top of him and rolled slowly into the street.

I swung my rifle against two more. Before I could draw a bead, however, they darted to safety around the corner behind The Danielle, abandoning their comrade.

The street was suddenly deserted. The only one in sight was the dead man. McGlynn worked his rifle bolt. We waited, scanning the street through our scopes. Neither of us said anything. One of the grunts behind the sandbags with us shook his head admiringly.

"That was one unbelievable shot!" he said.

A slight grin touched McGlynn's lips. It *was* a good shot.

We had almost given up on anything else transpiring when a compact red car came scooting around the corner from the street behind The Danielle. The way it arrived, racing its engine, reminded me of the circus clown act in which a backfiring Volkswagen roars into the ring and about two dozen clowns climb out of it.

Only, here in Beirut, no one was laughing.

The driver braked the red car next to the dead man and stayed behind the wheel, gunning the engine. Three armed ragheads looking like circus clowns scrambled out. Two of them ran directly to the fallen Shiite. They grabbed him by the arms and started dragging him toward the car. We would have let them go unharmed, except the third militiaman crouched next to the car and released a burst of automatic fire at us from the hip. Bullets thudded into our sandbags.

I had already cross-haired one of the Shiites dragging the dead man. He had been among those who had charged earlier from the cafe with rifle blazing. It was an easy shot of about 425 meters. I centered his chest. The bullet slammed him against the side of the car. Reflex action sent his AK sailing though the air. His body fell on top of the dead LAF deserter. His foot was banging oddly against the pavement when Corporal Frank Roberts, another STA sniper located in the adjacent position, spidered the red car's windshield trying to take out the driver.

I worked my rifle bolt, muttering, "Two down, three to go."

The red car stripped every gear in its transmission trying to get into reverse. Its rear tires finally caught and it boiled smoke. The two surviving ragheads in the street abandoned their dead and dived headfirst into the car, one of them first running alongside flailing his arms before he finally managed to get in. The car vanished backwards around the corner, still reminding me of the circus clown act.

This time there were *two* corpses in the street, one piled on the other.

A few minutes later, an old lady in a black shawl and a long black dress came out of the Ayatollah's poster building and started gesticulating angrily and shouting.

"I guess she wants that mess cleaned up," I interpreted. "Keep Beirut clean—bury a Shiite."

The unhappy Ayatollah stared threateningly from

above the old woman's head. I glanced at McGlynn. No words were needed. I could no longer resist the temptation. I shifted my rifle. The M-40A1 sniper rifle barked as people began running around in the street in helpless confusion and the old woman continued her caterwauling.

Cement dust exploded in a geyser from the poster wall, directly from between the glowering, hate-filled eyes of the Ayatollah Khomeini.

From America with love—*asshole*.

AFTERWORD

U‌p until after the Vietnam War, American military snipers went to war armed with modified-issue weapons or a combination of military issue and civilian hunting rifles. Snipers, often selected and "volunteered" haphazardly, were as makeshift as the weapons they used. Their skills were called upon when required, and then, after the sniper was no longer needed, he was shoved to the background like an embarrassing stepchild.

Official attitudes toward the sniper began to change in the 1970s when ranking military men began to see him as a legitimate and even honorable weapon. The American sniper's performance in Vietnam helped bring about this change in attitude, as did the fact that Warsaw Pact armies were assigning each of their platoons a trained sniper armed with a Dragunov SVD sniper rifle to complement the shorter-ranged assault rifles of the regular troops.

The U.S. Marine Corps established its scout/sniper school and designed a special rifle. Several Special

Forces men went through the Marine school and returned to the Army where they began pushing to replace the automatic-feed Match 14 with a bolt gun *and* to establish an Army sniper school modeled after the Marine example.

The Army was not emphasizing snipers to the degree the Marines were. It took until July 1987 for the Army to realize the value of selective marksmanship and establish its own sniper school at Fort Benning, Georgia. At the same time, the Army also constructed its "special rifle for a special job." Like the Marine M-40A1, the Army M-24 is a modified Remington 700. With minor differences, such as a Leupold scope and a flat black Kevlar stock instead of the Marines' Unertl scope and camouflaged stock, the Army M-24 and the Marine M-40A1 are the same rifle.

For the first time, both the Marines and the U.S. Army operate permanent sniper schools during peacetime. The sniper has come out of the closet.

"We've patterned much of our training on the Marine school," explained Staff Sergeant Ronnie Kuykendall, senior sniper instructor at Fort Benning.

The main difference between the Marine school and the Army school is that the USMC visualizes using snipers in multiple ways, from support of infantry on the defense or offense to interdiction for the purpose of selectively eliminating a target, such as when Carlos Hathcock went after the NVA general, while Army doctrine is more restrictive.

Kuykendall continued: "The infantry battalions will normally employ their snipers with the line companies on the FEBA (Forward Edge of the Battle Area). By complementing the short range of the M-16, we now have the capability of engaging enemy infantry at maximum ranges with precisely aimed single shots. That makes the enemy deploy early in the attack and reduces their numbers as they advance. The M-24 can outdistance the Dragunov and give us a distinct advantage that we did not have in the past. The man, the weapon, and the bullet become the most efficient and cost effective weapon we have on the battlefield.''

Captain Jim Land said it best in 1966 at his sniper school on Hill 55 in Vietnam: ''The most deadly weapon on any battlefield is the single well-aimed shot.''

For it made little sense, he noted, to drop a string of five-hundred-pound bombs, barrage an enemy with artillery rounds, or send in infantry spraying bullets at their opponents until one side struck down more than the other when the same thing could often be accomplished by one man with a single bullet—the deadliest weapon on the battlefield.

One shot—one kill.